My
Scandalous
Little
Rule Book

My Scandalous Little Rule Book

A Scandalous Guide to Sensational Success!

Jacquie Somerville

SelectBooks, Inc.
New York

This edition published by SelectBooks, Inc.
For information address SelectBooks, Inc., New York, New York.

First Edition

ISBN 978-1-59079-300-8

Library of Congress Cataloging-in-Publication Data

Names: Somerville, Jacquie, author.
Title: My scandalous little rule book : a scandalous guide to sensational
  success! / Jacquie Somerville.
Description: First Edition. | New York : SelectBooks, 2017. | Includes
  bibliographical references and index.
Identifiers: LCCN 2016004279 | ISBN 9781590793008 (paperback)
Subjects: LCSH: Success. | Risk. | Self-realization. | Satisfaction. | Life
  skills. | BISAC: SELF-HELP / Motivational & Inspirational.
Classification: LCC BF637.S8 .S63 2017 | DDC 158.1--dc23 LC record
  available
at https://lccn.loc.gov/2016004279

Manufactured in the United States of America
10 9 8 7 6 5 4 3 2 1

I dedicate this book to all the extraordinary women in this world who want more from life—more excitement, more adventure, and more fulfillment. May you find the courage to rock the boat, the strength to challenge yourself, the spirit to take a risk, and the wisdom to trust your intuition. You were born for greatness.

Regret for the things we did can be tempered by time;
it is regret for the things we did not do that is inconsolable.

—SYDNEY J. HARRIS, *Strictly Personal*

Contents

Acknowledgments

I owe a debt of gratitude to my husbands, lovers, friends, and nemeses—all of who have loved me, challenged me, questioned and supported me. My irritants have been my greatest teachers and my challenges have brought me closer to enlightenment. It has always been my desire to experience all that life has to offer: the good, bad, the ugly, and the beautiful. Everyone who has crossed my path on this magnificent journey so far has contributed to the rich tapestry that is my life. I thank them all. I thank my family for their love and support—my Mom, Dad, Garth, and Caro. It's not easy to support someone like me who pushes the boundaries of normalcy, and yet despite the resulting worry and the judgments you too may face for my decisions, your love is deep and pure.

I am deeply grateful for those friends of mine who do the same. You know who you are.

Introduction

The premise of this book is to urge you to stop being so cautious. Take a risk, achieve some major stuff, and have some fun! I'm not saying you should throw *all* caution to the wind—only some. You have to apply common sense. What I *am* saying is that we usually play this game of life much too cautiously, and in so doing, slip quietly and safely into the grave, never really having *lived*. We toe the line, conform, compromise, and conform and compromise some more until, meekly and carefully, we slide into the abyss of mediocrity.

The word "mistake" is overused in our society. I hate what it implies—that you shouldn't have done whatever it was you did—when really, aren't most of our "mistakes" an essential part of our own unique journey? When people tiptoe through life hoping not to make too many "mistakes" they ultimately miss out on actually **living**.

It makes me especially crazy when people refer to a marriage or a relationship that didn't last forever as a "mistake,"

1

or even worse, a "failure." Loving someone and following your heart is never a mistake, and nothing has to last forever to be perfect. Staying too long in an unhealthy relationship is an error in judgment that stems from not loving (and, therefore, not trusting) ourselves enough. We'll talk more about self-love in Rule 1, "Be Your Own Soul Mate!"

What *is* life if not the sum of our experiences? Do you sometimes feel that it's time for you to get out of your rut and live a little? Are you ready to break free from society's neatly prearranged molds, fly in the face of convention, and start to *experience* life? Since we are all going to die anyway, wouldn't you rather reach the end of your days exhausted, having no regrets, and with a smile on your face?

In the beautifully simple words of Jonathan Swift: *May you live all the days of your life.**

The key here is to weigh the odds and take calculated, informed risks. For example, throwing yourself out of an airplane without a parachute will kill you, but using a parachute and checking it carefully will more likely result in an exhilarating, memorable experience. Going home with a stranger while ignoring madly waving innate red flags could kill you, but tuning into and trusting your intuition will keep you safe.

Don't break the law. Live on the edge, but never cross over; breaking the law can really screw up your life and the lives of others.

I am not sitting here in pious judgment. I've been a bloody idiot many times throughout my life. Most of us have

---

* Jonathan Swift. *Polite Conversation* (1738)

been idiots at some point. We've all been young, but once we know better, we must do better.

I grew up in South Africa and lived in Johannesburg for a few years before immigrating to my beloved Canada. Johannesburg was a wild and dangerous place in the late '80s and early '90s (I believe it still is). I drove at excessive speeds, drank way too much, did both at the same time, and ran alone at dusk. I've had unprotected sex with strangers, jumped stone walls on horseback alone in the wilderness without a helmet, and I've lied, cheated, and tempted fate. I lived to talk about it, and for that I am extraordinary grateful. Not everyone is so lucky. I don't do those stupid things anymore. The kinds of risks I refer to in this book are those that require courage, not stupidity.

I've been married a few times, have immigrated twice, burned bridges, been fat, slim, broke, rich, loved lunatics, pushed the envelope, and lived to tell the tale. My past boyfriends, lovers, and admirers read like a roster at a UN Convention on Sexuality and the Modern Man.

Variety is unquestionably the spice of my life and I thrive on uncertainty. While I can learn from others how to incorporate more peace and stability into my life, it is my fearless approach to life's continuing opportunities that I want to share with you. It's been an exhilarating ride and I wouldn't have it any other way. I've gambled and won, gambled and lost. Never, ever, be afraid of losing at something that's worth trying—it is, after all, the potential to lose that makes winning such a thrill.

I must confess to times in my life when I failed to follow my own advice and passed up opportunities and adventures by saying no when I should have said yes. I remember turning down an outstanding trip to Argentina because of some crazy, self-imposed neurosis I was wrestling with at the time. I deeply regret that, but I don't regret any of the things I said yes to regardless of how challenging they turned out to be.

I'm not saying that you need to start screwing around, cheating, putting your life at risk, or ditching your family— hardly admirable solutions. There are myriad ways to break free from society's clutches. Stand for something, approach life with passion, shake up your sex life with your spouse, change your career, follow your dreams, write that book, quit your job, get super fit, trust yourself, start that business, go back to school whether you're thirty or sixty, travel, say "Yes!" more often, talk to strangers, open your mind, believe the signs, study personal-development, read more books, develop your own sense of style and wear it proudly, and above all, you **must** quit worrying about the opinions of others.

You may be saying, "Sounds great, but *how*?" Read on, and I'll tell you, but quite simply, you must apply common sense. This book is a combination of memoir and self-help. You may laugh and shake your head at some of my real-life antics, and at the same time you may be inspired to shake up your own life. My goal here is to inspire people to take more risk, to embrace uncertainty, and to challenge the status quo. Fasten your seat belts—you're about to find out how to get to the end of your days with a great big smile on your face, and no regrets!

Oh, and one more thing—read this and believe it: It is *never* too late. No matter what your age is, the time to make changes in your life is *now*. Don't waste another minute drifting along in the murky doldrums of mediocrity.

George Eliot said it best: *It is never too late to be what you might have been.*

You were born for greatness. Your time is now.

Be Your Own Soulmate

*To love one's self is the beginning
of a life-long romance!*

—OSCAR WILDE

An Ideal Husband, Act III

My Story: What's a Wanker?

A few weeks after our wedding, my beautiful husband and I went to a sex shop to pick up a few accessories. I heard moaning coming from the back of the store.

"Yikes! What is *that?*" I asked.

"There are little jack-off rooms back there," he said. "Guys come in here, rent movies and then jerk-off."

"*Really?* What's wrong with doing it at home?"

"They probably get off on doing it in a public place" he said.

Oh well, to each his or her own. I've always been perfectly happy masturbating in the privacy of my own home.

I was twelve when I stumbled upon the thrill of self-gratification, and I felt convinced that I had discovered something incredible and unknown to humankind. I figured if other people knew about it, I definitely would have heard of it by now, and wondered if I was the only person on the planet with this great power. I felt no guilt, but instinct told me to keep my discovery to myself. And so I did—indulging whenever darkness would allow. I looked forward to going to bed (I was a restless little insomniac), but now I had found something comforting and exciting that also helped put me to sleep. Yes, I loved masturbating.

One night when our family was on holiday in Kruger National Park, I shared a hut with my siblings, and my brother, in the process of telling a story, referred to some guy as a wanker.

"What's a wanker?" I asked.

"You mean you don't *know*?" he mocked, and refused to give me the scoop. I begged and pleaded and finally wore him down. Embarrassed, he explained to me that a wanker is a guy who derives sexual pleasure by playing with himself. Bang! went Jacquie, the Great Explorer. My secret was out—turns out everyone knew about this and, what's more, I was a wanker.

Now I am forty-eight years old, no longer an insomniac, married to a man whom I love deeply, and I am still a wanker. I've always been a bit of a loner, and some would say independent to a fault. When I was a little kid, I hated what I saw within my extended family—domineering men married to phenomenal, but subservient, women. I didn't get it. The women in my family were strong, loving, powerful, caring, intuitive, kind, fun, and intelligent. I wondered why they were ruled by people whom I felt clearly lacked many of those admirable qualities.

As I've gotten older, I admit to having found in those men some virtues I never recognized back then. I also have realized that these women had made their own choices based on what worked for them, but I was born a proud and tough little nut, and my observations made me prouder and tougher. I sought the company of animals and, above all, the company of myself. I spent as much time on my own as was humanly possible for a young kid within a traditional family of parents and siblings. I lived for time alone, and with our dogs at my side, I rode my horse for hours on end through the sugar-cane fields of my rural South African childhood. And I dreamed of a glamorous life on distant shores, of wealth and fame, of adventure and excitement, and of impacting lives.

My dreams for my future never included a husband and children of my own. In my dreams, my life looked very different from the path that society has carved so precisely for us over the centuries. Nothing about tradition appealed to me and I knew that I was different. I wanted to be unlike the wonderful women in my family, all of whom hid the bright lights of their full potential. I was not going to do that—I would not kowtow to anyone. I would be strong and successful and independent. I would make it on my own.

Through the years there came the endless questions from aunties, grannies, and other well-meaning adults, all of which I'm sure most of you are familiar with.

"Have you met someone special yet, Sweetheart?" And as you get older, "When are you going to get married and have children, my darling?"

My answer was always the same. "I don't want to get married. I don't think I want to have children."

"That's only because you haven't met the right one yet, my love! You will change your mind when you meet your *soul mate!*"

I don't want what you all have. I don't like what I see. I am different. I loathe compromise; I hate conforming. I want to be wild and free.

Slowly but surely, I started to feel that my being different must also mean being weird. I began to believe the opinions of others. Maybe they were right after all, and what I really needed above everything else in life was to find a soul mate. I would never be considered a success, at least not within my circle of influence, until I settled down with my soul mate and complied with tradition.

Nothing is celebrated quite like a wedding—not graduation, not professional or sporting achievement, not financial success, or other personal accomplishments. I set out to squash my non-conformist beliefs and in so doing moved further and further away from myself, my soul, my uniqueness.

And so it was at the age of twenty-nine that this hard-arsed, never-want-to-get-married-or-have-children kid, surrendered and got married. And whom did I marry? A gay man. Why the hell? Because I think, subconsciously, I had found a way to check off that all-important item on society's checklist, and to do it in such a way so that it couldn't possibly last or result in children.

I felt that I would be deemed a failure if I didn't conform. In order to pass the "normal" test, I had to add that check mark to the marriage box. My choice of husband, naturally, shocked the shit out of "normal" so who was I kidding?

You see, the really interesting thing is that no matter how hard you try to squash the spirit of who you are your authentic self eventually finds a way to bite you in the arse. Destiny demands your attention, or else your life can get quite fucked up in the process. Looking back, I wouldn't change a thing—this is my journey and every euphoric peak, crazy dip, and deep, dark valley has been and continues to be essential. There is, however, a vital lesson in all of this for me going forward and for generations (particularly women) to come.

If I were to idealistically rewrite this part of my story, I would describe having stood up to the pressure of society, and rather than finding a man at any cost, focusing on finding myself and my purpose on Earth. Only then could I present a complete, well-loved, and fulfilled person to the world, able to attract genuine love from others of the same ilk.

At forty-six, I married again, and while my husband and I are at different stages in our lives, ages, and careers, his love is deep and pure, and he doesn't care to pretend. I'm much more secure within myself and with my purpose and place in this beautiful world. My love for him is, and continues to be, for no other reason other than **love.** I feel no fear and know that I'm whole with or without a spouse. I look forward to whatever the future brings. I've found freedom in self-love and in my belief that the Universe is unfolding as it should.

I am, without a doubt, my *own* soul mate! And yet, I'm not saying that I have this down to a fine art—not by any means. I occasionally still exhibit spectacular displays of insecurity and self-doubt. This is a journey—one that begins with self-awareness. The goal is uncompromised self-love, but it takes a while to get there! Are you ready to start your journey? You begin to change your life at the moment you decide that you are!

~*The Lesson*~

You are the most important person in *your* world. How you feel about yourself determines your *entire life*, including the quality and quantity of love that you experience with others!

In recent years many women have asked me, when referring to their own lives, "Is this all there is?" The question ignited my passion and I felt fiercely compelled to find answers to why most of us go through our entire lives never feeling the full force of a thrilling life. I found that reason: we are all (especially women) taught from a young age to find our happiness through other people and things. We're never taught that loving ourselves is of prime importance. Instead, we're taught that loving ourselves is selfish and conceited. We spend our lives being plagued by doubt and insecurities—including those of us who appear outwardly confident.

As I see it, our inability to live extraordinary lives comes from our failure to love who we are—not merely as individuals but as a collective group of beings across the planet. Arguments, fights, wars, disputes, stalemates—would they even exist if we all, individually, loved ourselves enough to let others simply be? We would feel free from judgment, hatred, and intolerance. Constantly trying to change people and point them to our way of thinking is a result of our own insecurities. We continually seek external validation and feel validated only when we "win."

So what do we do about it? I want to start a movement—one that spreads across the world and changes lives, a movement that revolutionizes the way we think and the way we'll raise future generations. The name of the movement? BE YOUR OWN SOUL MATE! Stop this obsession with seeking happiness beyond ourselves. We must stop the obsession with finding our soul mate in another person. The key to true happiness? BE YOUR OWN SOUL MATE!

I hasten to add that I love men, and I'm crazy about sex, romance, and love; so it's not as though I'm trying to diminish such delicious and important aspects of life. It's just that if we spent as much time working on truly loving ourselves as we do on finding a "soul mate," then we would have the self-confidence necessary to live an extraordinary life. And if we spent as much time empowering kids to be confident and secure within themselves, as we do in finding someone else to love us, we will have raised a successful and happy generation.

It is our constant pursuit of joy and happiness through others that causes chronic insecurity, limitations, and heartache. Yet, this is what society embraces and teaches us; it is particularly true for women and girls. As a culture, we are obsessed with weddings, love stories, romance, and "finding our one, true soul mate." Girls are still raised with Sleeping Beauty, Cinderella, and Beauty and the Beast. Don't you think it's time to change the message?

The determination to "find" that soul mate so that society can celebrate and congratulate us becomes an all-consuming pursuit, and, naturally, leads to misrepresentation. We slip further away from being our true selves. We put on a front to market ourselves successfully. We find the soul mate and then, in many cases, spend the rest of our lives trying to hold on to him or her. And, sadly, so many of us never become what we were truly meant to be.

Shakespeare said it best:

> *This above all: to thine own self be true, And it must follow, as the night the day, Thou canst not then be false to any man.*

When you are you own soul mate, you are no longer plagued by insecurities. Criticism, deformation, and rejection will no longer render you paralyzed, unable to function and move toward your dream life. You will be able to put everything into perspective and move forward with strength, excitement, determination, and wonder!

Imagine life when you're so completely sure of yourself and your own value that you aren't affected by the things people say, or don't say, do or don't do to you. You come to realize that if you feel hurt, it is only because of that fragile part of you known as the ego; once aware of this, you will be able to break free from the hurt.

Be your own soul mate!

Loving yourself above all else is truly the miraculous answer to living a magnificent life. Imagine!

When you love yourself fully, you trust yourself fully. When you trust yourself, you also trust the Spirit, the Divine Force that resides within you—your intuition. When you trust your intuition, you are no longer hesitant or afraid to follow it. Imagine the possibilities!

Ralph Waldo Emerson said: *Self-trust is the first secret of success.* We hear so many "secret" principles of success but . . . self-trust as number one? I think he was on to something.

When we love ourselves, we trust ourselves; when we trust ourselves, we banish fear and doubt. What holds us back from living the life of our dreams? Fear and doubt. Without them we are able to move mountains. Can you imagine what you would do if you were guaranteed to succeed, i.e., if fear of failure and fear of rejection were removed from the equation? I'll bet you would set out to accomplish your definitive idea of success!

Being loved by others is **not** the most important thing in life. Finding your true purpose and getting to know and love **yourself** is the most important thing! When you do that, you will be successful in *all* aspects of life, including beautiful, external, and passionate love!

The big question is: "How?" How do we dismiss a lifetime of indoctrination, overcome negative self-talk and self-doubt, and start to love ourselves fully—to believe with profound knowledge in our own worth, contribution, and uniqueness?

I have developed a program called "Be Your Own Soul Mate! 7 Steps to Grabbing Life by the Balls and Living with Love, Wealth, Adventure, and Freedom."

What follows is a short summary of the program. Please go to www.jacquiesomerville.com to obtain the program in its entirety. My course will change your life forever. You will feel empowered to love yourself fully, and in so doing, bring love, wealth, adventure, and freedom into your life!

Here is an overview of what you will gain from the **Be-Your-Own-Soul-Mate** program:

1. You! Right now . . .

We analyze where you are now and where you want to be. All change starts with acknowledgment, and we cannot change what we refuse to admit. The road to becoming your own soul mate starts with analyzing your current belief system and figuring out where it came from. When we realize that our beliefs about life, society, and what's good or right for us, are neither carved in stone nor necessarily the gospel truth, but rather have been passed on to us by other fallible human beings, we can begin to change them. We can start to challenge the status quo, to question, to stand up for ourselves, and to quit the obsessive concern with what others will think or say. Who made up these rules anyway? Other human beings just like us. That means humans—just like us— can change them!

2. Imagine the Fabulous!

Here, we go deep into your dream life. We create the excitement of possibility. This process is essential in the

Be-Your-Own-Soul-Mate journey because it relates to the issue of creating desire. It's your big *why*. When you get super excited about something, you make every effort to make it happen. There is tremendous power and excitement in possibility and desire.

3. Be a Control Freak!

There is tremendous strength, power, and momentum that comes from self-respect and from taking charge of the things within your immediate control. We have to respect ourselves in order to like ourselves. We have to like ourselves in order to love ourselves. When we love ourselves, we trust ourselves. Take charge of what is within your control; the universe will conspire with you and good things will begin to happen!

4. Get Your Fab On!

This is similar to Step 3 in terms of being the best you can be and taking charge of things within your control, but this time it's about your own body. We delve into diet and exercise and what generates the energy needed to accomplish dreams. It's not about taking away what we love; it's about adding the stuff that's great for us. (I'm a self-proclaimed hedonist. I hate deprivation.) We talk about style and fashion and image. When we feel we look good on the outside, we also feel better about ourselves and project great vibes out to others! We become confident, joyful, and sexy women. We get our FAB on! This step is about doing what it takes to feel sexy, confident, and worthy because you know you're doing your absolute best. You feel as though you can conquer the world—you're on fire! That's when you attract the people and circumstances that will change your life for the better.

5. You'd Better Believe It!

We work at removing the negative shit , that we uncovered in Step 1. It's about mantras, affirmations, and continuing education as well as visualization and focus. We teach the concept that your thoughts and beliefs create your life and the importance of taking responsibility for your past, present and future. We teach the importance of faith. There are no coincidences. There is a Universal Force, a Creator, a tie that binds. This force works with us when we do all we can to be the best we can be. That's a powerful combination!

6. The Roadmap Less Travelled

We build your Dream! We put a plan in place—a roadmap to the brand new you. This step deals with beliefs, goals, your burning desire, and the big "why." And it's about ACTION!

7. Gain Velocity and Celebrate, Baby!

We examine daily habits and rituals, and deal with the setbacks that life sometimes throws at us. It's about building the muscles that make us strong and powerful. It's about consistency and persistence and taking a moment to celebrate YOU! This step will solidify your power. You will go out into the world with courage and enthusiasm, free from fear of failure and rejection, and free from worrying about the opinions of others! You can live a life of love, wealth, freedom, and adventure! You can live *your* dreams. *You* are your *own* soul mate!

Go to www.jacquiesomerville.com for more details on this simple, but life-changing program. You will be able to go into great detail and begin to develop self-respect, find your purpose and worth, determine your own greatness (yes, we *all* have it), and in so doing, become your own soul mate!

There Is Divine Intelligence—Believe It

You can do very little with faith, but you can do nothing without it.

—SAMUEL BUTLER

"Rebelliousness," *Notebooks* (1912)

My Story: Tom

Like a lot of people in my generation, I was raised with religion—in my family's case, Christianity, and we identified with being Anglican. I dreaded church; we lived in a small rural community of farmers, so services were held only every second Sunday. I hated Sunday school. The guy who ran it is one of those people who speak very differently to children from the way they do to adults. Even when I was eight or nine years old, I remember thinking that he was a complete idiot, and there was no way that I was going to buy into anything that this nerdy nincompoop had to say.

At age eleven, I went to boarding school at a British-style, all-girls establishment, that could have been the setting for a sort of 1970s Dickens novel. The dorm floor had that waxy, institutional red polish and our resident ghost, Sticky Feet, who roamed the corridors at night, kept company with hoards of giant, marauding cockroaches.

After every holiday we had our heads dunked in paraffin because someone always brought back nits to the dorm. We always blamed the Zambians. The place was hot and sticky, the food meager and disgusting, and the prefects scared the bejesus out of me. It's no wonder that I suddenly wanted God on my side. During "Fellowship," held once a week in a tiny room with a piano, we would sing, clap, sway, and stamp our feet. It was the closest thing to letting loose that we were ever going to see in that draconian establishment, so I signed up. Hallelujah!

High school was not a whole lot different, and I relied on Bible study for hope and comfort, not to mention the fact that it was held next door. We could actually leave the school grounds for an hour or so—a crime otherwise punishable by expulsion. And again, it provided one of the few opportunities for waifs locked up in an all-girls nunnery to sing, dance, stomp, and clap.

The minute I left the constraints and shackles of boarding school, I dropped God like a hot potato. My dance partners were no longer restricted to God and girls. I discovered boys at university, the strange, enigmatic creatures, that were so much fun to dance with, flirt with, and tease. I could drink, swear, and skip class. I was free!

And so it was that I left Him/Her/It hanging for the next fourteen years. I graduated from university, travelled around the world, began my career, immigrated to Canada, and got married and divorced. I no longer identified with being a Christian, and over the years my experiences, along with the diversity of the people I met, led me to the ultimate conclusion that the dogmatic, exclusionary, and judgmental nature of organized religion was absolutely not for me. I never paid much attention to what belief I might replace it with, and I got on with life as a physical being. I felt no need to delve into the possibility of a Spiritual Force—that is, until a pivotal experience lead to an epiphany at the age of thirty-one.

My friend, Tom, was exuberant, kind, charming, thoughtful, and handsome and reminded me of James Dean. He was the life and soul of any party, and would give you the shirt off his back if he thought you needed it. He was one of a kind, and in 1996 I learned he was dying of AIDS. He had been in deep denial for too long, and by the time he sought medical help and the necessary drugs, it was too late.

When Tom had a few months, or maybe even only weeks, to live, he was moved to a hospital about five hours' drive from Vancouver to be closer to his parents. They called me when the end was imminent, and I went to say goodbye.

My friend's skin clung to his skull and his eyes were dark and deeply sunken. He looked like he was already dead. His skin was covered with lesions. We sat in awkward silence. I didn't know what to say to someone who was about to die, and he didn't know what to say to someone who was staying behind. We had been such close friends, but beating around the bush made us feel like strangers in that weird moment.

"How are you?" I finally asked, in thoughtless desperation. It was as though anger woke him from the dead.

"How the hell do you *think* I am? I'm scared shitless."

"Don't get angry with me," I shot back. "I'm scared too and I don't know what the hell to say under the circumstances."

Our honest exchange instantly brought back comfort and familiarity. We relaxed and fought back tears. He became frail again and lay back motioning to me to come toward him. I leaned in on his chest and tried to hug him without touching his tremendously painful skin.

"I'm going to miss you," he said.

My lips quivered. We held on to each other for a minute.

"I'm going to miss you too," I said. I left his dark hospital room and when I got out in to the corridor, I sobbed inconsolably. I drove back to Vancouver and within the next twenty-four hours, Tom was gone.

There are so many joyful reasons why his memory lives on within me and will do so forever, but the most profound lesson that he taught me was the one from his deathbed. Tom was not a religious man, and like me at the time, he didn't pay much attention to the spiritual side of life. We had both toyed with the idea that maybe this was it—when you die, you die, end of story. And yet, on his deathbed, in an unplanned, intuitive moment of pure instinct, he said, "I'm going to miss you." If ever there was an unsolicited and pure moment that solidified for me, beyond a shadow of a doubt, that we live on in some way, in some form, that was it.

If he wasn't going anywhere, how could he miss me? And if, when you die, you die, how *would* he miss me? It is my unyielding belief that intuition (that spiritual power residing in all of us) indicated to him, without explanation, that he was going to live on somewhere, somehow. How else could he *possibly* miss me?

From that moment, I became aware of the presence of the spiritual force that exists within all of us, and from that moment on I became certain that all things are possible. I now know absolutely that I am guided and supported. This faith enables me to tune in and *trust* and in so doing, take the risks necessary to live an extraordinary life.

I realize that when our time is up, we will live on somehow, and mine is not to figure out how, but simply to feel content with the knowledge that we do.

The feared, vengeful, and masculine God of my youth had dissipated and had become something more ethereal—a spiritual presence, the Creator, a force for good that guides my life.

~*The Lesson*~

This is what I have learned: Our job on this earth is not to spend our days stewing over the meaning of life and living in fear of a bigoted dictator in the sky, or living in fear of the unknown. Our job is to become all that we, in this physical form, have been put here to be. Our purpose is to find, and *live,* our purpose! It's that simple. And we find our purpose by tuning into and trusting the divine force that resides in all of us, our intuition.

Faith is critically important. Without it, we would live without hope or become strangled by the force of ego. I have known many financially very successful people who believe that they stand alone, with no guidance from any force greater than themselves. Aside from their massive egos making them too insufferable to be around, they are also paranoid and very unhappy, constantly seeking that elusive person, place, or thing they believe will finally bring them happiness.

With faith comes hope, without which we could never excel, and at worst, we would drown in despair. But faith offers us much more than hope.

> *Faith is the ability to see the invisible, to believe in the incredible, and that will permit you to do what the masses call impossible.*

I first heard this powerful quote from Bob Proctor, though I've since seen versions of it attributed to others.

Faith in no way discounts responsibility—we are responsible for our own lives. Faith without action is useless, and without faith, most of us would not take action in the first place. In life, we must take the actions necessary to create change or to run with an opportunity. Ask God/the Universe for guidance, take action on everything within your control and then, only then, "let go, let God."

Once I have done everything ethical and legal within my power to make something happen, and it still doesn't work out, I trust and believe that it is, quite simply, not meant to be. I love this quote from *Desiderata*, the brilliant prose poem written by Max Ehrmann in 1927:

> *You are a child of the universe, no less than the trees and the stars; you have a right to be here. And whether or not it is clear to you, no doubt the universe is unfolding as it should.*

While I am not a proponent of organized religion, I acknowledge that for many the structure, rituals, dogma, and rules are very helpful and comforting. But here's the rub: Teaching that God is a dictatorial ruler who, with a flick of a hand on Judgment Day, will condemn people to fry throughout eternity, not only allows hatred and bigotry to be justified, but compels people to *fear* God. And when people fear God, they can perform indescribable atrocities in his name, supposedly to save themselves from his wrath.

I recently watched an interview of four men from the Central African Republic who had been kidnapped as young children by warlord Joseph Kony to be made child soldiers. These kids were told that this was "God's war," leaving them deeply fearful and forced to comply. Serving in Kony's army meant committing horrific acts of terror and violence, but being on God's bad side was even more terrifying for them.

Let us, instead, perpetuate the idea that God/the Great Spirit guides us as a non-judgmental and loving force for good. Would the world not be a much better place?

Believing in a spiritual force for good, or whatever you choose to call it, gives us hope, comfort, power, guidance, support, and strength. We are able to trust ourselves, take risks, find our purpose, and achieve astonishing success. *Believing* seems like a no-brainer to me.

The German physicist, Max Planck, won the Nobel Prize for Physics in 1918. He was an important scientist who originated quantum theory and forever changed our understanding of atomic and subatomic processes. This quantum theory and Einstein's theory of relativity are considered the most important in 20th Century physics. The dude was a *scientist*—among the most noted in history, and here's what he said about the existence of a Creator:

> All matter originates and exists only by virtue of a force which brings the particle of an atom to vibration and holds this most minute solar system of the atom together. We must assume behind this force the existence of a conscious and intelligent mind. This mind is the matrix of all matter.
>
> From *Das Wesen der Materie (The Nature of Matter)*
> Speech in Florence, Italy, 1944

~*Tips on Finding Faith*~

⊚ Look to nature. There is tremendous evidence of the existence of the Creator in nature. Marvel at its beauty and wondrous workings and you will begin to feel connected to a force greater than yourself. Such breathtaking intricacy and beauty could not be an accident.

⊚ Feel tremendous *gratitude*. Be grateful every day for all that you have in this extraordinary life—from the air you breathe, the people you love, the roof over your head, the food you eat, and the puppy that makes you smile. Be grateful, and you will start to feel joy in your heart and a connection to your soul. Make gratitude a habit by writing in your journal each morning at least five things you feel grateful for that day. This simple act can change your attitude and, in turn, change your life.

⊚ Spend time alone. I mean really alone—not even in the company of your TV, computer, book, radio, or phone. The Universal Spirit resides within *you* and not on its own little continent in the sky. You need to be quiet and still in order to tune in to it.

⊚ Meditate even if you don't really know what to do! Sit quietly for ten minutes every day. Breathe deliberately and listen to your breath; marvel at the extraordinary workings of the human body. Sometimes, I listen to guided meditation, and I especially love Dr. Wayne Dyer's "Getting in the Gap" and "Meditations for Manifesting."

⊚ Don't stress over what you call "It." From God to Buddha or from The Universe to the Source, it really doesn't matter. What matters is that you believe.

⊚ Read. Here are my own favorite spiritual books that feed my soul and bolster my belief:

> *Inspiration* by Dr. Wayne W. Dyer
>
> *Making the Shift* by Dr. Wayne W. Dyer
>
> *Wishes Fulfilled* by Wayne W. Dyer

The Power of Now by Eckhart Tolle

A New Earth by Eckhart Tolle

The Monk Who Sold His Ferrari by Robin Sharma

The Seven Spiritual Laws of Success by Deepak Chopra

Spiritual Solutions by Deepak Chopra

Make a decision—the decision to believe. Don't waste your life questioning and postulating on the existence of God. You can choose to feel supported and guided and trusting of yourself, or to feel alone and skeptical, doubting yourself and constantly offended by your fragile ego. At the end of the day, it really is a simple choice: tune in and trust.

There is a source that we are all connected to, a tie that binds. When we tune in to our source, we are guided and supported.

Believe it.

Rule

3

Say Yes!

You've got to jump off cliffs and build
your wings on the way down.

—RAY BRADBURY

From interview distributed by AP, November 1990

My Story: Love and Lust in the Produce Aisle

I know for certain that there are no coincidences in this beautiful and challenging world. On March 30, 2012, I said yes to a young man in a California grocery store and for the first time in my life, I found true, unconditional, unadulterated, pure, passion-filled love.

I was selecting cheeses for a dinner party, and the young man was handing out bruschetta samples. He said, "Hi," stared at me for a while, and as I walked off, he said, "You are very beautiful." What? What did he say? Shit! He looked really cute and no more than twenty-two. While I'm fortunate to have been complimented by strangers over the course of my life, at forty-six years of age I felt a bit shocked to hear this from someone so young. I blushed and said, "Thank you." As I started back up the next isle, he smiled and asked, "How are you?" I said, "I'm great, now that you just made my day."

I was picking out produce when he came to find me. He rushed up to me, shook my hand, introduced himself, looked at my left hand and said, "So you aren't married." I laughed and he disappeared. He was a risk-taker—he didn't care that he could have been fired. I might have complained and, besides, there were cameras all over the place. Hitting on a patron was no doubt an employee no-no, but he was so determined to know me and I was curious to find out why.

He was back at his sample post near the front of the store, and I waved goodbye as I left the checkout. I had a strong feeling that he would find a way to connect with me one more time before I drove away, and if he didn't, I would go back and hand him my card. A man willing to put his job on the line to connect with me was someone I wanted to know more about. I'm attracted to guts, confidence, determination, and courage; besides, he was tall, handsome, and engaging.

Sure enough, after a couple of minutes, he followed me outside and made his way toward me, pretending to collect shopping carts along the way. He reached my car and handed me a white paper napkin with his name and phone number scrawled across it in black ink.

"Call me," he said.

"No," I replied. "You call me," and I handed him my card.

I laughed out loud as I drove off. *What the hell was that all about? A Casper looking for his J-Lo?*

His first text came before I even got home. "You from here?" (My Canadian area code prompted this question.)

Me: "For part of the year."

Him: "How much time do I have?"

Me: "About six weeks."

Him: "OK. I get off work in a few hours. Can I call you?"

Me: "Yes."

He called when he got off work. "Want to get together and have some fun?" he asked.

Well, yes, now that he put it that way. I still wasn't too sure what it was all about, but since my forties have been a decade of rather enjoyable sluttiness, I felt game for anything.

"You'll have to come over to my place," I said. "I can't leave my dog alone."

"I can do that—I have a car," he replied.

There is always a certain amount of risk involved when one has a dog that can't be left alone. Last-minute spontaneous get-togethers have to happen at home, and I dug deep to see if my gut was throwing out any red flags. The coast seemed clear, but I did lock up my jewelry and wallets in the safe, just in case curiosity had clouded my usually trusty instincts.

I felt a fleeting moment of doubt when the doorbell rang. What the hell am I going to do with this young man? He's a total stranger from a different generation; he works as a grocery-store clerk and I had just invited him over to play in my fancy holiday house. What am I going to say? I needn't have worried.

"Hi!" he said, with intoxicating enthusiasm. His smile was broad and white and perfect; his eyes were wild and alive. He seemed so proud of himself. Then he wrapped his gorgeous, big arms around me and embraced me with an emotional hug so intense it was as though we had known each other our whole lives. I knew in that moment that the evening would unfold as it should, and I knew that this man was unique—his soul was special. I melted into him.

"I've already got a double vodka going," I said. "What would you like to drink?"

"Well, I guess I'll have what you're having," he said. "I don't really drink. My grandfather is a Sioux Indian, and he's an alcoholic. Besides, I don't like it much." And with that, he began to tell the story of his life; it flowed out of him in a no-holds-barred, cathartic, whole-hearted purge, one shocking detail following another.

The Beautiful Man was born in California. When he was two years old, his German mother was killed in a car accident, and when he was five his father went to prison in Mexico for drug dealing. The Beautiful Boy and his sister were sent to live with their paternal grandmother in Mexico. After two years, it had become too much for her, so she decided to keep the girl, but to send the Beautiful Boy to live with an aunt back in California.

And so began his troubled and itinerant childhood, defined by abuse, neglect, hustling, and panhandling. At age fourteen, he was arrested. He became a ward of the state and was sent to military school.

At eighteen, he went AWOL just before being discharged. He was caught eleven months later and thrown into L.A. County jail to fester for a year. I have no doubt that the experience solidified his hatred for the system, for authority, and for the rule of law.

It's no surprise that he followed in his father's footsteps and ended up in prison, albeit for a different crime. He had looked up to his father, as young boys do.

He married at twenty-three while in prison (after getting his girlfriend pregnant just before entering), and now had an eight-year-old son. His divorce was about to be finalized. He showed me scars from police-dog bites and rubbed my finger over two bullets still in his leg, a leftover reminder of a childhood and adolescence best left forgotten.

I grilled him with questions, wanting to understand a life so radically different from my own. My childhood was defined by love, support, security, safety, discipline, and guidelines. The Beautiful Boy lived a childhood completely devoid of all such basic childhood needs. And I wanted to know what prison was really like. Surely a pretty boy would be fodder for the sexually deviant inmates? How did he stay safe?

"I've never met anyone who has been in prison. When did you get out?" I asked.

"A couple of years ago." He pushed the barstool back, stood up, and engulfed me in those sexy, bad arms again. Then he put his hand under my chin, lifted my face, and softly, sensually, perfectly, and spectacularly kissed me. Within minutes, we were naked in the pool, crazy with raw passion and lust. Rock that boat.

The man could kiss. Holy hell, he was sexy! And here's the thing: lips are sexy, but a wide-open, wet mouth, and a ramming tongue is not. I already knew about being swallowed whole, like Jonah and the whale, and the feeling of drowning before being swallowed is even more terrifying. This man, my young, troubled ex-con grocery boy, could teach the world how to kiss, and there are many men I've known who should attend this class.

At 10.30 p.m. we made scrambled eggs. "What do you want to do with your life?" I asked. "I mean, are you going to slice meat in a grocery store for the rest of your days?"

"No way," he said. But he clearly didn't know what he wanted to be when he grew up. "You just don't understand. It's really hard. People don't give people like me a chance. No one else will hire me."

He certainly needed another job. At a pitiful wage and part-time hours, he was living well below the poverty line. I found myself wondering if it was a matter of time before he turned to stealing, perhaps drug dealing, and back to prison. We all know the statistics; now they made sense to me.

The Beautiful Man didn't seem to realize that he had legal and legitimate options that could improve his life, that he could be or do anything, and that he was free to imagine and dream. And that's why I felt we had been destined to meet—not because I thought that I could save or change him, but because I could suggest things to him that no one else ever had.

"And how old are you, anyway?" I asked. "You look about twenty-two."

"Well, how old are you?" he said. "Not that it matters."

"I'm not telling you, but I'm pretty sure I'm older than you think I am," I replied.

"So am I—I'm twenty-nine." He showed me his driver's license. "Now, based on what you just said, I think you're probably thirty-eight; at first I thought maybe thirty-five."

"Perfect," I said. "Let's leave it at that." Thank God for Botox.

He wanted to spend the night with me. "I like to sleep alone," I said, and at 1:00 a.m., I asked him to leave, but not before inviting him to join my dinner party the next night.

"I have four friends coming over. They're all gay men and I hope that you'll be okay with that because if you're not, we might as well end this now." His response was positive and I was excited.

When I awoke the next day, I went into full detective mode. I needed to find out if everything that Mr. Beautiful had told me about his life was, in fact, true. I have seen so many of those *Dateline* shows where gullible women, desperate for love, get duped by conmen doing brilliant jobs of winning them over after eliciting sympathy. It's not as though I'd write the guy a check anytime soon, and I was certainly not desperate to find a man, but I didn't want to hang out with someone whose intentions toward me were anything but truthful and pure.

And so it was that he was telling the truth.

He joined my friends and me for dinner, and that night I fell in love with him. Some thirty hours after meeting the Beautiful Man, I no longer wanted to sleep alone. He stayed, and eight months later we were married. There were compelling reasons for us to get married and to get married quickly—I will cover these in a later story. But eight months after saying "Yes" to a troubled, complicated, beautiful, poverty- stricken ex-con seventeen years my junior, in a grocery store, I said, "I do," to him in a chapel in Las Vegas. My life became a lot more challenging, chaotic, passionate, interesting, honest, and overflowing with love.

There were many times during the course of those eight months that I felt overwhelmingly frustrated and helpless. Throughout many nights, I would stare at his peaceful face while he slept in the comfort and safety of my bed, and I would think about all he had been through. I felt engulfed by sadness as well as by pure, unadulterated love. I wanted so badly to wave a magic wand and make it all better.

And many times during those eight months, I doubted him, tested him, and dug deep into my soul to look for answers. I constantly challenged him about his future, his attitude, and about contribution. He told me that all he needed was to feel loved—sweetly and naively believing that love is enough.

"It's so much more complicated than that," I said. "Love alone is not enough to sustain a relationship. Both parties need to bring more than just adoration and passion to the table. People need to eat, they need shelter; they need hopes and dreams for the future, and they need to contribute." Inadvertently, I began to lecture, so desperately wanting him to see that despite his past, he *could* have a charmed life. He just had to *believe* it.

"Now you're being judgmental again," he would say.

Well, yes. Goddamn it, I so badly wanted him to see that he had to change the way he looked at the world, before the world he looked at changed.

"Just love me," he said. "Just love me and give me time."

And so I did, and I do. While I still get frustrated and impatient when I see all the potential in him that he fails to recognize, I realize that a lot of my frustration comes from the fact that I know that *I too* have untapped potential. It's like looking into a magnifying mirror, and that motivates me to expect more of *myself.*

Yes, he teaches me just as much as I teach him. He has brutally challenged my notion of unconditional love. While I can give him food, shelter, and material security, he has nothing to give me but love, and unbridled passion. That is difficult for me. Apparently I do attach conditions and expectations to a romantic partnership.

However, I have discovered that it is impossible to love such a man when you have conditions and strings attached to the love. So, when I am frustrated beyond measure, I stop and remember that the universe brought the Beautiful Man into my life for a very good reason.

He has taught me that there is tremendous freedom in staying wide open and truthful with our emotions; he does not care to pretend. I still build walls, and so far, he still has the patience to help tear them down. He has taught me that for love to be real, we have to be vulnerable. He has opened my heart and shown me real love, and I'm beginning to come around to the idea that maybe he's right. Maybe pure and simple love *is* enough.

"Oh, and by the way," I asked one day, "what did you mean in your text on the day that you met me—the one where you asked how much time you had?"

"I wanted to know how much time I had to make you fall in love with me," he replied.

Mission accomplished.

~The Lesson~

So much of this rule is based on my belief in knowing that there are no coincidences in life. We need to say "Yes!" more often to what our extraordinary universe offers us. Occasionally, we have to say "No," if only so that we get to know ourselves better, stay sharp and tuned in, or to be taught a quick lesson. I've learned something very important about the power of a simple "No"—it's enough by itself. You needn't explain yourself further to anyone. If you aren't feeling it, say "No!" Period.

Once you believe in yourself as your own soul mate, and no longer make decisions based on insecurity, ego, or pleasing others, *and* you're tuned in to your instincts, it's time to say "Yes!" a lot more often.

Don't be bound by what you "should" do or say or by old beliefs and paradigms deeply engrained in your psyche. They continue to hold you back and keep you from recognizing opportunity, seeking a new career, getting rich, finding love, having great sex, travel, laughter, and adventure—and from *living*!

When someone unusual asks you out on a date, by all means, meet him or her in a public place, but say *yes*. When someone you know buys you a plane ticket, but you have no vacation time and no money, figure out a legal way and say *yes*. When you are offered an opportunity to begin a new career, be interviewed, speak in public, move to a new city or country, write an article, go on a road trip, or mentor someone despite feeling unprepared—figure out a way—and say *yes*. When presented with an opportunity to challenge yourself, better yourself, push yourself, and you feel paralyzed by fear, say *yes* anyway. When life presents you with opportunities, trust yourself and jump—you *will* build your wings on the way down!

A word of caution when there is money involved. I would urge a very large amount of skepticism when offered an opportunity in exchange for a significant amount of money. These prospects are rarely conducive to spontaneity. Do your due diligence, but be inclined initially to pass.

I am experiencing heart-busting love and being challenged to love unconditionally for the first time because I said *yes*. I said "Yes!" to a situation that many people, including my past self, may well have fled from because of judgment and fear. Such pre-conceived notions can prevent us from experiencing some of the greatest love and joy that life has to offer. The lesson is this: When people and opportunities cross your path, give them a chance; trust your intuition, and say "YES!"

Remember that nothing has to last forever to be perfect. There are people, circumstances, and opportunities that cross your path for a reason—sometimes for only a fleeting moment of joy or to teach a quick lesson. My life coach, Clarity, offers the quote: "People come into your life for a reason, a season, or a lifetime." Longevity does not define perfection. Plan for the future, but live in the moment.

My Beautiful Man crossed my path because I'm at a stage in my life when I have so much love to give—love kept suppressed for fear that vulnerability would leave me weak and pathetic. I fell in love with someone who *needs* so much love and who has a knack for opening my usually closed heart.

It is not lost on me that a big part of my Beautiful Man's attraction to me perhaps is a subconscious desire for a mother figure or for guidance, and that a big part of my attraction to him may be the subconscious desire to be needed. That's OK—we attract what we need at any given moment in our lives, and when that comes along with the added bonus of an abundance of love and passion, how fabulous is that?

The timing of events presented to us is controlled by the Universal Force—one greater than ourselves that we are all a part of; that is, the Spirit Guide I talk about in Rule 2. Walking into that grocery store at the moment I did on that day was no coincidence. My job was to know that, to trust, and to say *Yes!*

~*Tips for Knowing When to Say "Yes!"*~

⊙ Accept that there are no coincidences in this world. There is a reason for everything.

⊙ Be your own soul mate! See Rule 1.

⊙ Don't confuse spontaneity with stupidity. To be spontaneous successfully means to take a moment to tune in to your Spirit. See any little flags waving? Don't ignore them. See more on this in Rule 8, "Heed the Signs!"

⊙ Be very skeptical when asked to exchange money for opportunity. Do your due diligence.

⊙ When you know and trust someone and the person offers you a free (or at least affordable) opportunity, it's a no-brainer—say, "*Yes!*"

⊙ Learn to know the difference between fear and healthy intuition. If it's fear of the unknown that holds you back, say "Yes!" anyway. If genuine red flags are waving, say "No!" How do you know the difference? By being aware of the fear imposter, by questioning yourself and your motivation, and by practicing. Practice saying "Yes!" more often in no-risk situations; pretty soon, you'll become better at trusting yourself and saying "Yes!" to slightly crazier opportunities!

⊚ Write down the pros and cons when faced with an opportunity. Very often, most of the cons will be based solely on fear of uncertainty. Be honest with yourself. Is uncertainty holding you back, or is there a genuine reason for concern?

⊚ Think—but don't *overthink!* How many times in life have you missed opportunities because you thought of every possible negative scenario that had minuscule odds of ever coming to pass?

Everything happens for a reason. Please don't ignore this essential fact. Don't leave the universe hanging in disbelief only because you turned down, over and over again, what it presents to you with divine perfection. Next time, say *YES!*

Life Is Too Short
for Boring Sex

*Sex is as important as eating and drinking and we
ought to allow the one appetite to be satisfied with as
little restraint or false modesty as the other*

—MARQUIS DE SADE

L'Histoire de Juilette, ou les Prosperites du Vice, pt 1 (1797)

My Story: 50 Shades of Kink

As I mentioned in the first chapter about Rule 1, Chapter 1, my lover took me to a sex shop shortly after our wedding. These joints always seem sleazy. This one stood tucked behind an industrial parking lot and was filled to the rafters with porn movies, rubber shlongs the size of horse dicks, gags, whips, paddles, beads, cuffs, and clamps—a veritable treasure trove of smut.

"What do you want, baby?" my husband asked out loud.

"SHHHH!!!" I said, keeping my eyes to the ground. "This is your deal, darlin', you pick."

Great sex is made even better with accessories, and we loaded up with vibrators, lube, dildos, cock rings, anal beads, and nipple clamps.

"Which ones do you want?" Loverboy asked.

"Shit, damned if I know—I've never had anything shoved up my arse before. Not sure I want to start now—and as for the nipple clamps, aren't they all the same? Get those $7.00 ones made in China."

We raced home, jumped into bed, and tore open the packages. During the throes of accessorized passion, my man reached over, grabbed the nipple clamps, and released one on my boob.

"OWWW!" I screamed at the top of my lungs. "GET IT OFF, GET IT OFF—OWWW—GET IT OFFFFF!!!! He hesitated, and I screamed even louder. It's not that my hands were tied, but I felt paralyzed with pain and unable to release myself from the brutal thing.

"It's because they're cheap," he said, unclamping me. Really? You get what you pay for—even with nipple clamps in a porn shop? Who knew? And, besides, I would think that a looser coil spring would cost less than a tightly wound one; actually, that's not the case.

I eventually read *Fifty Shades of Grey* to see what all the fuss was about, and I have to say that it left me feeling positively pious. I always thought of my sexual fantasies as relatively perverted, but apparently not. And it isn't the book itself that I found shocking, but the fact that millions of women are turned on by Christian Grey. If I went home with some dude who opened a door to a medieval torture chamber, I'd run for the hills. Even more certainly, if he beat me on the arse so hard that I couldn't sit down, I'd likely be the one to end up in jail. I'd *never* put up with that nonsense.

There is a strip joint a block or two past the sex shop and we went there a few weeks later. I strolled in, holding my lover's hand and trying to appear nonchalant—*so* unconvincing. My husband, on the other hand, knew the bouncer, the manager, and a couple of the strippers. We were clearly in his world, and I loved to see him take control.

'Who do you like, baby?" he asked. We watched the girls selling themselves up on the stage.

"What for?" I asked.

"For a lap dance, of course," he said.

What the hell? I don't do girls. But, OK, since I had to pick. "I'll take the older one with the sexy boobs," I said.

Turns out I'm a boob girl; interesting—it was news to me. Who knew that I would get off on sexy girls grinding up and down and across my body, whispering in my ear, caressing me, all while I peer around them at my husband indulging in the same?

"Just relax, baby, I love to watch you," he said. "Touch her." Oh god, no.

Three different girls rubbed me up and down over the course of the evening. The young, petite blonde with the soft, perfect body did nothing for me—too young and too pouty. Her attitude put me off. I kept coming back to the older woman with the sexy boobs. She's experienced, mature, and intuitive, and she has no chip on her shoulder. She knows that she has choices and she chooses this. She knows, too, that while she dreams of other things during the daylight hours, at night she gets off on being seductive, desired, and chosen.

I watched my favorite girl grind up and down over my husband's body. I watched him stare at her beautiful tits and I watched his sexy hands move up and down her back. *Fascinating*, I thought. *I'm not jealous or concerned—I'm turned on.* Here, in the strip club, his self-assured, experienced cockiness made me want him even more.

Sex was mind-blowing that night—exactly how I like it. It was hard, raw, enhanced with toys, passionate, wild, and with just a hint of madness.

The next morning I felt closer than ever to him. Strip clubs stayed on our agenda. It's not that I had discovered a hidden attraction to women—I remain straight—but spending time with the man I love, and want, in a sexy and salacious environment, is great for our sex life, and anything great for our sex life, is really, really good for our relationship.

~*The Lesson*~

When it comes to sex with your partner, push the envelope a little, get out of your comfort zone and, above all, be *confident*.

Here's a thought about sex: It's frigging delicious and a barometer for so many other aspects of life. Great sex requires self-confidence, imagination, creativity, and an open mind. If it's not great for you, chances are you lack some of these qualities, and that affects other areas of your life. In this rule, I use sex as a metaphor for so much more.

The biggie here is self-confidence, isn't it? How many women can relate to worrying about their thighs in the throes of passion? I know all about this; I've been a pretty bad lover myself in years gone by, and it always boiled down to a lack of self-confidence and being consumed by someone else's opinion.

What a great place to start working on your confidence— in the privacy of your own bedroom, and with the support of the one you love! It's the perfect place to begin pushing that envelope, and what's more, it's a stress reliever, an endorphin inducer, and a whole lot of fun! It's the ideal place to bust out of your rut and blow your partner away (pun intended) with your newfound kinkiness.

Here's the interesting point about pushing the envelope. I'm not suggesting that anyone do anything illegal, unethical, or what they may be morally opposed to. Having the courage of your convictions is essential and admirable. What I *am* suggesting is that you evaluate your situation honestly. Are you using excuses to hold yourself back when the truth is that you merely lack confidence or are fearful of the unknown? Question your motivation. To live an extraordinary life requires that you regularly step out of your comfort zone, and a great place to start is in the bedroom.

Force yourself. Push the envelope. What are you waiting for? We pass this way only once. Lack of self-confidence in all aspects of your life will lead to a lifetime of regret. Ride roughshod over the bullshit and self-doubt you tell yourself every day, and replace it with strong, positive affirmations. I likely have never met you, but I know something about you. You are unique. There are now more than seven billion people on the planet. The best guess is that some 108 billion people have been born over the course of human history, and get this—there has never been another you! That's no accident.

Hold your head high—you deserve to be here. The world is lucky to have you; your lover (or future lover) is lucky to be with you, and life is too short for lack of confidence to hold you back.

Life is too short for boring sex.

~*My Sex Tips*~

⊚ Write suggestive notes to your partner (it's often easier to write something than to say it face to face).

⊚ I love writing notes in red lipstick on the bathroom mirror—for when he wakes up in the morning or gets back from work. Start with a simple "I Love You," then move on to "I Want You, Baby!"

⊚ Buy your partner a "naughty" gift, something a bit out of character for you. It can be a great start to your new, cheekier image! The very first gift that my husband bought me soon after we started dating was a vibrator. And the gifts keep coming.

⊚ Take a trip to the sex shop together. If it's not something you do regularly, you'll feel like a naughty kid doing something you shouldn't, and that's always a thrilling feeling. If nothing else, you'll enjoy having a good laugh.

⊚ Invest in a few accessories: start with a good vibrator, but don't stop there.

⊚ Keep the mystery alive! I remember an interview with Angela Lansbury when she was asked what her secret was to a long and successful marriage. "Never let him see you struggle into your pantyhose!" I love that. By all means, be yourself and be real with your partner, but remember to be sexy too.

⊙ You need to *feel* sexy first. Eating crap and overindulging leads to the antithesis of feeling confident and sexy. I hate to sound like a stuck soundtrack but a healthy, wholesome diet and daily exercise will work wonders for your sex life and your confidence in general.

⊙ One word, girls: **Heels.** Not only does wearing them make me feel sexy, but I have yet to meet a straight man who isn't turned on by a towering pair of stilettos. Surprise him in heels with a short silk robe left open in the front; make love with the shoes on. Delicious!

⊙ I asked my husband for his No. 1 tip for great sex, and this is what he said: "When you're with the person you love and trust, say "Yes!" to something a little out of your realm of normal. Having a partner who makes a habit of saying "No!" in the throes of passion is a major turn-off. Who wants the same old boring sex routine every time? And if you say "No" too often, they'll eventually lose interest and stop trying. If your partner is more adventurous than you, experiment with it."

◉ Stop focusing on your "faults." Most often, it's only *you* who notices them! When someone mentions a zit on his or her face, ninety percent of the time it never would have been noticed if it hadn't been pointed out. We spend too much time and energy worrying about things that no one else cares about, and if they do, so what? Take heed of the great quote that is often attributed to Dr. Seuss: *Be who you are and say what you feel, because those who mind don't matter, and those who matter don't mind.*

◉ If you're single (or not) you already know what I think about the game of solitaire: play with yourself. You will reduce stress, get to know yourself better, fine tune your imagination, figure out **what turns you on, and you'll sleep like a baby.**

Like most things in life, self-confidence is a choice that you make, and as with most decisions after they've been made, you have to work at them. Decide to be confident from this moment forward. It's no one else's decision but your own, and caring what others think hurts no one else but you. Decide to challenge your comfort zone from here on. Starting now, decide to have sex with the lights on.

Rock the Boat

All life is a chance. So take it!
The person who goes furthest is the one
who is willing to do and dare.

—DALE CARNEGIE

My Story: Simon

I was born a seventh-generation, white South African on November 13, 1965, a mere seventeen years after apartheid had been written into the rule books and twenty-five years before its demise. When I was a child I believed that Nelson Mandela deserved to be in prison. The government controlled the media, and we were told that he was a terrorist. We were told that he would be released from prison if he denounced violence as a method for fighting apartheid. As a kid, I never realized that to do such a thing would be swapping one prison for another. As a true leader, he had to do what was right for the people and not what was easier for himself. Neither he nor the people of South Africa could ever be free as long as apartheid existed.

I travelled to the United States and Western Europe when I turned twenty-one. My travels exposed me to what life was like where people lived in relative harmony and where the press was free to show the ugliness of apartheid. My exposure to life in the West changed the way I looked at my motherland and changed the views I had held until then. I had always known that apartheid was wrong—my parents had taught me that—but I felt quite fine burying my head in the sand and going about my life without rocking the boat. I supported the view that change needed to happen very slowly. But I had finally grown up and developed my own thoughts and views about life. I asked questions, argued, took a stand. I no longer parroted the opinions of others. Change was inevitable and it was right. I began to look at it through the eyes of those who were oppressed—it had to happen sooner rather than later.

I don't have radical blood flowing through my veins. I speak out on issues that I feel strongly about, and take action in passive ways such as fundraising or donating. I've never been a protester or a marcher, and never really stuck my neck out too far.

However, there have been times in my adult life where I look back and regret not having acted in a more radical way and standing up in strong protest of clear wrongs. I was plagued by such feelings when I read Nelson Mandela's book, *The Long Walk to Freedom*. I struggled with guilt but found redemption in the words of Maya Angelou: "When you know better, you do better." Her wisdom has helped me to understand and forgive myself, and to have compassion for others who are equally misguided.

I returned to South Africa in September of 1988 under duress. My country felt so stifling and artificial to me now that I knew more of its hidden truths. I had tasted freedom and wanted to stay in the United States. At the time, amnesty was granted to illegal aliens who had overstayed their welcome by five or more years. I had been more than willing to give it a try—overstay my welcome and fly under the radar for five years doing odd jobs here and there—but this would be over my Dad's dead body.

"Get back here," he had ordered. "You have obligations and student loans, and besides, you did not get a university education to drift for the rest of your life!"

I moved to Johannesburg and got a "real" job as a marketing consultant, and later, as a district sales manager for one of the largest automobile companies in the country. I had to call on the dealers in the eastern section of what was then the Transvaal Province (the old Transvaal is now split into a number of different provinces: Gauteng, Mpumalanga, Limpopo, and the North West). By far, the majority of small towns that I called on were extremely politically conservative; in other words, radically racist. It should go without saying that there were, and are, many wonderful people of all colors and origins in these towns, including Afrikaners, and my intention is not to paint everyone with the same brush. I was shown tremendous kindness and hospitality by many Afrikaans families in my district. The stories that I tell, however, are those that impacted and changed me, as well as the course of my future, forever.

One day I stopped at a small store outside a tiny town just east of Johannesburg to pick up some water and something to eat. I walked toward the counter and saw an elderly black man standing, holding his wares and waiting to be called up to pay. The middle-aged white Afrikaans shop-keeper motioned to me to come ahead of the old man.

"No, sir, he was here first," I said. The shopkeeper continued to motion angrily at me, saying nothing. Intimidated by his self-ordained forceful authority, I obeyed. I walked out of the store with tears in my eyes. I had witnessed an old man's dignity being eroded that day, and I hated it. I wish that I had refused to do business with the shopkeeper. I should have put my goods on the counter and walked out. I should have, but I didn't. I allowed myself to be intimidated into keeping the peace. Why didn't I rock that boat?

We knew our dealer in the eastern town of Standerton was a member of Andries Treunicht's Conservative Party. The company was anxious that he keep his politics and his dealership separate. It was critical that the company not be associated with overt racism, especially at a time when the trade unions were wreaking havoc with strikes and work stoppages across the country. Even a company as progressive and pro-active as ours was not immune to such intense action by the labor force. At the time, the anti-apartheid movement had very few other peaceful tactics to utilize since the ANC and other groups remained banned organizations.

The salesman at Standerton was Pieter. I hated him for his politics, but he was fiery and wild and passionate, and when he flirted with me, there was a danger and an intensity that was oddly appealing. I had to do business with him. I wanted him to sell as many cars as he could. The numbers reflected on me and I wanted to do well. I also had to make sure that he kept his racism to himself when he represented the company, and that references to politics in the dealership were kept at bay. There was a large photo of Treunicht on the wall. I tried for years to get that thing taken down. I took all of these concerns as far up the ranks as I could go, but stripping a dealer of the franchise was not easy.

I believed that the best way to get any sense or reason from Pieter would be to have a good relationship with him. What was I thinking? Of course, there was no reasoning with him; his beliefs were ingrained in the roots of his boots. He knew where I stood on the issue of apartheid, and I would argue intensely with him. He loved it and would trivialize my points by laughing them off.

One day, I was sitting at Pieter's desk discussing his new vehicle requirements for the following month, when two young black men walked into the dealership. They proceeded to closely examine a car standing on the showroom floor. Pieter yelled, "HEY"! and pulled out a revolver from his desk drawer. He waved it at them and placed it on his desk. I was overcome with rage and disbelief. I could barely breathe as I told him that as long as he had our company's name on the door, he would not discriminate against potential customers. He laughed at me. I could only imagine the hatred in the hearts of those young men—to be treated that way simply for existing. I walked out that day feeling sad and scared for the future of my country and my future in it.

It was not long before I left my beloved, sad, messed-up, beautiful country that I had another pivotal incident in

Standerton. I had gone to the fax machine in Pieter's office to send something to head office. There was a fax coming through, and I couldn't help but see it. It was a call to all conservative members to arm themselves and get to the Western Transvaal town of Ventersdorp where President F.W. de Klerk would give a speech. Ventersdorp was another bastion of racism; in fact, it was the hometown of the loathsome leader of the Herstichte Nationale Party, Eugene Terreblanche. Right-wing Afrikaners felt outraged and betrayed by de Klerk for his negotiating with the "enemy," i.e., Mandela and the ANC, and for trying to affect a peaceful solution for the inevitable change that was coming. On the night of the speech, protesters stormed the hall and innocent people died. Pieter was one of the protesters. It was all too close to the bone for me.

Into this fray entered my friend Simon.

He was a Tswana man from near Port Elizabeth in the Eastern Cape. The company's head office was also in this area. If I remember correctly, the corporation awarded him a scholarship to attend college in the United States. He graduated with a Bachelor of Commerce from the University of Minnesota in St Paul. After returning to our head office for a while, he was transferred to the regional office in the Transvaal to gain experience in "the field." The company had high hopes for him.

Simon and I become friends right away. Despite the different colors of our skin, we had much in common and looked to each other for support. He was a black man in a white-dominated, conservative industry and I was a woman in a male-dominated, conservative industry. We both had university degrees when the majority of our colleagues did not. We had both experienced life in the United States and reveled in our shared stories. We hung out together, confided in each other, and laughed a lot.

Simon had an extraordinary sense of humor, and next to my Granny Barbara, the most infectious laugh I had ever known. He used it as his coping mechanism, and he needed one. The odds were stacked heavily against him. If Simon made even the smallest error in judgment on the job, or was late for a meeting, it was because he was black. On the other hand, if a white guy arrived late for a meeting, it could be assumed that he'd had a problem with his vehicle, or other such perfectly legitimate excuses seen as beyond his control. No one ever fucked up just because they were white. I wondered why I was the only person who noticed.

When I pointed this out and defended my friend, everyone thought I was a delusional drama queen making up shit that didn't exist. I kept at it and was laughingly told, "Hey, Punda* shut up man—no balls, no brains." I felt that the best way to deal with the guys would be to abuse them right back, play them at their own game, flirt with them, laugh with them, and then do well at my job. I realized that I was more likely to be heard and respected if I appeared not to take myself too seriously.

---

* *Punda* – derogatory South African slang meaning female.

Simon tried a similar tactic, using his incredible sense of humor to make jokes and laugh off as much as he could. We had never discussed tactics, but as with me, experience had taught him that this was the only way to gain respect and acceptance. It didn't work as well for him, though, and I realize now that as a female amidst all the testosterone in the automobile industry, I had a distinct advantage over him. Despite all they threw at me, the guys enjoyed having me around, but many of them didn't want Simon there. They desperately clung to the old guard, and he represented the inevitable changes so threatening to them. And so they refused to cut him any slack.

He would laugh at racist jokes so that he would fit in. He would laugh at stereotyping so that he would be seen as one of the boys. He would laugh at their overt racism thinly disguised as bar stories, and yet all the while, the undercurrent of suspicion, blame, and intolerance remained so strong that it seemed certain to pull him under. And, one day, it did.

When I immigrated to Canada in 1992, Simon was still a district manager at the regional office in Johannesburg. I visited him there the following year when I returned home for a family event. He still appeared to be the same joyful man that I had known, but he confided in me, without offering details, that he was having some personal difficulties.

Simon and I eventually lost touch after he left the company. It was always extremely difficult to get any information about him until another trip back in 2005. I found out from a former colleague and friend that Simon had died the previous year. I was thirty-nine years old at the time. We had been about the same age. I was told that he drank himself to death. For the first time in my life, I felt heartbroken.

It is shattering for me to believe that one of the most jovial and positive people I had ever known died in such despair. I don't know all the reasons why Simon's life spiraled out of control. When I think back to the comments and silent undercurrents that made up a constant part of his life as a one who was an early recipient of the policies of affirmative action, I know that they played a significant role in the breaking of a man's spirit. I have often felt that if I'd been there, I could have saved him. Unrealistic, perhaps, but that knowledge doesn't make the feeling go away. I tried to find him many times, but he was a proud man, and I wouldn't be surprised if he didn't want his friend to see what had become of him.

When I feel overwhelmed with sadness, I listen for his laughter.

~*The Lesson*~

Here's the thing about rocking the boat and taking a stand: If you don't, you will likely be plagued by regret. Regret will hold you back from ever being fully you, from believing in your own greatness, and from accomplishing your own version of spectacular success.

Live your life so that you will have no regrets. Stand up strong and proud in the face of adversity, and rock the boat.

If I had stood by quietly listening to all the racist comments and jokes and innuendos in our office without saying anything, I would still be filled with regret. My friend's death would not just have made me extraordinarily sad, but it also would have been completely debilitating. My colleagues enjoyed my company, as I did theirs, for the most part, but when it came to racism, they all knew where I stood. Whenever Simon was bad-mouthed or blamed, they knew, beyond any doubt, that I would *always* take his side. I wish that I had done more.

I also learned a valuable lesson about forgiveness. I had to forgive myself for believing what I had believed as a kid. I had to forgive myself for defending, with all good intentions, the indefensible. Forgiveness is essential, but we must not carry on with the status quo. When we know better, we must *force* ourselves to do better. Burying our heads in the sand and being afraid of stirring the pot will lead to a lifetime of regret.

Living without regret, and standing by our values, are important keys to living an extraordinary and fearless life.

We are *passionate* when we are prepared to take a stand and rock the boat, and we cannot achieve greatness without passion.

Where do you need to rock the boat in your own life? I refer not only to taking a stand on behalf of others or for society in general. I mean the things you know that you should do to help you bust out of your rut but that you aren't doing because of fear and discomfort. What will you regret down the road if you don't suffer minor discomfort now?

A year, or five years from today, what will you wish you had had the guts to face up to? When caught in a passionless existence, you *must* rock your own boat. Throw a spanner in the works. Shock the hell out of your comfort zone. It's often tough, and sometimes treacherous, but the short-term crapola will far outweigh a lifetime of regret.

Don't be wishy–washy in your approach to life. Be gutsy and fearless and passionate. Never be afraid to take a stand. Have the courage to push the envelope. You will reach the end of your days without regrets. You will have had a well-lived and meaningful life.

Rock the Boat. You'll be glad you did.

~Tips for Rocking the Boat~

- Comfort is overrated—it can lead to regret.

- Fear is overrated—and usually unfounded. Challenge yourself every day.

- Growth comes from challenge and discomfort. If your life is stagnant, rattle your cage and force some growth! You will reach new heights.

- Are you scared of learning new things? Enroll in a class. Afraid of being alone? Go away for a solitary weekend. Afraid of flying? Book a trip.

- Are you proud of whom you are? Take a stand.

- What makes you mad and sad? Take a stand; speak up. Do something about it.

- What are you putting off (that you know will change your life for the better) just because it will cause you short-term pain and discomfort?

- Be courageous. Face your fears head on. Courage is a decision.

- Do something that scares you—or at least makes you uncomfortable—every day.

- Forgive yourself for ignoring stuff from the past that needed your attention. You know better now so force yourself to do better.

- Approach life with *passion*. You will stand out. Be bold.

- Pay no attention to the haters. Author Gloria Tesch reminds us, "Behind every successful person lies a pack of haters! I love my haters!"

- Ask for guidance from your Spirit. Know that you are supported, and know that you have what it takes to deal with the challenges that come from rocking the boat. Stay connected with your source.

Do you need to rock your own boat? Challenge yourself. Pick one aspect of your life that is stagnant and shake it up! You deserve to live without regrets.

Burn Your Bridges

Often the difference between a successful man and a
failure is not one's better abilities or ideas,
but the courage that one has to bet on his idea,
to take a calculated risk, and to act.

—DR. MAXWELL MALTZ

Psycho-Cybernetics: A New Way to Get More Living Out of Life

My Story:
A Suitcase, a Tennis Racquet,
a Phone, and a Futon

W hen I was a new immigrant to Canada, I passed out in Safeway one day. I was spending my first few weeks with a kind and lovely young couple who knew my Dad. They also were originally South African and the guy was a doctor.

"I wonder what's wrong with me," I said to him that evening.

"Jacquie, you have just immigrated to a new country. You don't know anyone. You have no friends or family here. You have no home. The world is in recession and you have no job or any prospects for a job. This constitutes severe stress. You passed out from severe stress."

OK, so subconsciously I was a fuck-up but, consciously, I felt excited and optimistic about my new country and my future. I had arrived at a delightful stage in my life—my twenties—when most things feel like a great, big exciting adventure. Bad things happened to other people, not to me. I was in that youthful and blissfully ignorant state when the entire world may be affected by something, but I stayed completely immune. Thousands might be fired, but I would be hired.

I hasten to add that this attitude did not come from the knowledge that I had something special to offer, like some advanced degree in a rare subject, a brilliant brain, looks to die for, or legs extending to eternity. No, it came from pure, blissful, youthful, ignorance. What a gift!

It was with that same attitude and optimism that I had left my motherland. The application for residency to Canada involved a long and arduous process, despite the fact that I had had an immigration lawyer working on my case. Many months after sending in the paperwork, an interview was granted with the Canadian officials to determine my talents, motives, and compatibility. The letter confirming the interview was clear. **"The fact that you have an interview date by no means grants you residency in Canada. You may still be turned down. Do not sell your possessions, give up your home, or quit your job."** So, naturally, I sold my possessions and gave notice to my landlady and my boss.

I burned my bridges.

My Toronto lawyer, Mr. Greenfield, chose to work with the Canadian Consulate in Buffalo, New York, and in hiring him I agreed to fly the 8,250 miles from Johannesburg to Buffalo for my interview. All the while, of course, I was constantly reminded that I might still be turned down after such a long and expensive undertaking. But I believed that I had horseshoes up my arse, so I booked a passage on a Greyhound bus scheduled to depart from Buffalo the morning after my interview. I would arrive in Toronto a few hours later.

My plans were coming together. I had an interview date. Check. I had a flight to Buffalo, New York. Check. Handed in my notice. Check. Told everyone who would listen that I was moving to Canada. Check. Sold my possessions. Check. I had a bus ticket to Canada. Check.

Then another notice arrived in the mail just ten days before my flight to Buffalo.

> Dear Jacqueline,
>
> Your interview for May 2, 1992 has been postponed. The Canadian Consulate in Buffalo, NY, is under renovations. For your own safety, your interview is now scheduled for September 10, 1992.
>
> Once again you are reminded that you may still be turned down for Canadian Residency. Do not sell your possessions, your home, or quit your job.
>
> Sincerely,
The Canadian Consul General

My safety? My arse. Didn't they realize what a massive blow this was to my plans? How could they put my future on hold for four entire months? I was panic-stricken. I called Greenfield. "I have everything planned. My non-refundable flight is paid; my company has granted me leave of absence and arranged for someone to work in my place. (I didn't tell him the full story about giving notice and counting my chickens before they had hatched.)

How can they do this to me?" I squealed, squawked, and pleaded.

"OK," said Greenfield in exasperation. "Write a dissertation spelling out all the very important reasons why the consulate should make an exception in your case."

I wrote a classic sob story. I was highly motivated and did whatever I could to convince any reasonable human being that postponing my interview until September would be an extraordinarily cruel, and, in fact, would have a very debilitating effect on me. I faxed it to Greenfield.

One night at about 10:30 p.m., I heard the phone ringing as I opened the door to the house in Johannesburg that I shared with a friend. That time of night could only mean one thing: Canada calling. I dropped my bag and keys and sprinted to the phone.

"Jacquie? Greenfield here. Proceed to Buffalo."

Those were his exact words. I'll never forget them as long as I live. I was over the frigging moon.

"Pardon all the boxes and construction mess," said the very stiff Consul General who accompanied me through the hallway. I wore my most professional-looking business suit and Lady Di heels (it *was* 1992).

"Don't hurt yourself." It seemed like much ado about nothing, but I made sure that he knew how grateful I felt for the exception they had made for me.

He asked me a few questions about my career. I had a briefcase full of documents touting my importance and my accomplishments. I had been a mere district sales manager for the auto company, but after my presentation, you would be forgiven the assumption that I had been the president of a large multinational company. He cut me short and asked why I had chosen Canada. I had prepared a flawless answer—I was ready for anything asked of me. There was no way I'd screw this up. I was good. I was prepared. And I had no Plan B.

The entire interview lasted ten minutes. Mr. Consul leaned over the desk, shook my hand, and said, "Welcome to Canada."

"That's it?" I asked. "I'm in?"

"You're in," he said. "Good Luck"

The next day I boarded the Greyhound with my immigrant papers and crossed the border at Fort Eerie, Ontario. My first step into my new country was as a landed immigrant. There was no going back. I had no doubt that I was going to make it.

Make it I did, but not without being challenged, scared, and pushed to my limits.

I met with Greenfield in his Toronto office the day after my interview. He had told me to come by to pay the final balance of his fee and said that he would give me some pointers for life in Canada. I handed him the cash and he thanked me and stood up to walk me out.

"Um, you said that you would give me some pointers," I stammered.

"'Yes, yes, OK, what do you want to know?" I pulled out a city map and asked which areas a single, unemployed girl should live in. He circled a few places quickly and stood up again. He reached over the desk and shook my hand. "Thank you, and have a nice life," he said, quite sincerely. He was all about business—the consummate professional who had accomplished everything that needed to be done for me.

While staying in a tiny room for $19 a night at a boarding house run by friendly Jamaican ladies, I spent a week wandering the streets, reading the newspapers, and trying to get my bearings. Toronto seemed like Johannesburg—a big concrete jungle—only a whole lot safer. Some kind people suggested that Vancouver was likely more my kind of place, so I boarded a plane.

The view from the air of the West Coast of Canada took my breath away. Ah, yes, this looks beautiful. I think I'll live here. What did I have to lose? I had no home, no job, no friends, and no possessions save for one suitcase and a tennis racquet. I could plop down anywhere and make a go of it.

After spending a few weeks with the doctor and his wife, I found a place to live and felt excited. It was down at the beach, the price was right, and I would share the condo with its owner, a dark, handsome thirtysomething guy who swore that he spent most of his life in Colorado. He wouldn't be there much. Perfect. I bought a futon and my very first cordless phone. I felt so very grown-up and very "First World." I had my own phone line in my bedroom—essential for all the calls that I would be fielding for interviews, I thought.

I applied for every job advertised that looked in any way, no matter how remote, related to my prior experience or education. Even a common word was good enough for me. One of the ads was for a district sales manager for a large direct-sales cosmetic company. The fit seemed too good to be true. I had left my job as a district sales manager for a large automobile company in South Africa, just weeks prior to applying. Cars to cosmetics—how different could it be? They called for an interview, then another, and another. Weeks rolled into months. All the while, I applied for jobs and attended the odd interview here and there, but nothing panned out. I had been told by other immigrants that I would often hear, "But you have no 'Canadian' experience" thrown at me. I thought that sounded pretty silly but they had been right—it happened over and over again.

Meanwhile, my roommate ended up being a nutcase. He spent way more time in residence than he had promised. One day our phone lines crossed. He stormed into my bedroom screaming at the top of his lungs.

"HANG UP THE PHONE!! HANG UP THE FUCK-ING PHONE. HANG IT UP NOW!!" He stood in the doorway of my bedroom with his phone in hand. His face was purple and he shook with rage.

The lunatic proceeded to tell me that I had fucked up his life because his girlfriend had heard my voice on the crossed line and accused him of having an affair. Now she was furious with him and didn't trust him and it was all *my* fault. He threatened me. I immediately felt extraordinarily vulnerable. I was being attacked irrationally and red flags waved in alarm. No rational person would ever react like this over something so inane. And like many violent, irrational people, he was full of remorse about the incident the next day. This guy was dangerous and I had to get the hell out of there.

He left town a few days later and I launched into a full-scale, urgent apartment search. I found the perfect little place: a one-bedroom rental in a five-story walk-up a few blocks from the nut house. Real estate is very expensive in Vancouver, making the demand for cheap rentals extremely high. The old Austrian owner told me that he liked me but that someone else had beaten me to it.

"Please, please," I said, in desperation. "I'm living with a roommate right now who is violent and I honestly fear for my life. Please reconsider my application. I'm very afraid."

He and his wife Anne were kind people and they were worried about me. They gave me the apartment despite my precarious employment status and my lack of references. They knew what it felt like to be a new immigrant. God love them.

Before the lunatic returned from Colorado, I packed up my futon, phone, tennis racquet, and suitcase, and moved into my own little place. Now one problem was solved but I still didn't have a job. I did some babysitting for $8 an hour, and I tried my hand at being a restaurant hostess for $4 an hour, all the while sending out resumes and applications at breakneck speed and determination. I received no response.

One day I came across an ad from an electronics company promising the world to salespeople. During the interview, I found out that the job paid commission only and that we would receive a $1,000-a-month draw that we would have to pay back with our first $1,000 earned in commission. We had to train for six weeks before we could sell and they would pay us the draw during training, but again, we'd have to pay it back through commission. Yikes—it sounded like a horrible deal to me, but I was desperate. "I'll take it," I said.

The training took place in Port Coquitlam. I boarded a bus at 6:30 a.m. every morning and made four bus changes that included a two-hour journey through Vancouver's toughest neighborhood to arrive at the school from Hell. We started each day with a group yell. One of the new recruits was elected to open the yelling. "HOW'S EVERYBODY DOING TODAY?" The group had to reply with equal force, "SUPER, FANTASTIC!!" If your yell fell short of the required decibel level, you were ordered to do it again.

Nowadays, I understand their thinking, but back then I thought this morning ritual was weird, unsettling, and cultish. I hardly felt super or fantastic. I was a poverty-stricken immigrant who, as it turns out, hated selling stereos. However, in the midst of my self-pity, I sat next to a guy who diligently studied amps and receivers in the lunchroom. He was from Singapore, and a fully degreed engineer. I felt humbled. At least this bunch of yellers was giving us immigrants a chance.

I completed the training and moved to one of the stores and onto the sales floor. I had all that draw money to pay back so I had to hurry and sell something. I celebrated my first big sale of a full stereo system after a week or so. Two days later, the customer returned the entire thing. I got on the train after being on my feet for ten hours and realized I had just worked that day for minus $53. I couldn't justify those hours at six days a week and at that rate of return. I needed to turn my search for a "real job" into a full-time endeavor, and so I quit.

By now, my application with the large cosmetics company was approaching the six-month mark. One night I received a call from John, the division manager. He told me he thought I'd probably be good at the job, and that the fact I was South African was an asset as he had had great experiences with my fellow citizens. But he couldn't risk hiring me when a former manager with a proven track record was due to return to the company. I felt my knees weaken.

After numerous interviews, tests, and days spent out in the field with managers, I had given this job application my all over the course of many months. And while I had continued to apply for everything available, nothing else had panned out, and I had no other irons in the fire. It was 1992, and every day the newspaper headlines roared on about layoffs. I had enough money for only one more month's rent.

Giving up and going back to South Africa was never an option for me. I would make it in my new country or die trying.

The night of John's call had been the closest I had ever come to cracking. I remember so clearly breaking down, and in floods of tears, scrubbing the bathroom floor of my little Kitsilano apartment. I wallowed in my misery for a while and then, despite the fact that I was in the middle of a spiritual vacuum, I got down on my hands and knees and admitted to God that I was in serious need of help. I pleaded for some and woke up the next morning with renewed determination.

I honestly don't remember how much time passed between John's phone calls. It may have been a few days or a few weeks. All I know is that his second call changed my life. He said that not hiring me had been troubling him; he had recently fired a manager and now he wanted to offer me the position.

I did John proud and finished my first year as one of the top three new managers in the country, with more success to follow. When he left the company, I stood up at the farewell lunch and thanked him for taking a chance on me, and for changing the life of a new immigrant. I don't know where he is now, nor do I know where I would be had he not given me the break that I so desperately needed. What I do know is that *something* would have panned out. But I will never forget him.

Yes, immigrating is a stressful and challenging undertaking, not for the faint of heart, and damned if I didn't do it again twenty-one years later.

And to make it really, *really* work, you mustn't ever have a plan B.

~The Lesson~

My tenacity paid off. Because I had left myself without the option of failure, my determination level was through the roof, and I approached each hurdle with ferocity. We make things happen in this world when we're up against the gun. Most of us are raised with the lesson "Never burn your bridges!" To that, I say burn away. Keep people on your side but burn the bridges that would enable you to beat a hasty retreat. You accomplish great things if there is no plan B.

Aren't most of us raised with the notion that if you pursue your dreams, you must "have something to fall back on?" It's all so vanilla, so bland, so conceding. This mindset dilutes your belief. It dilutes your resolve and highlights doubt. If you want something bad enough, you will go for it with every fiber of your being. If your need and want is diluted, you most likely will fall short of your dreams.

Want a new car? Why not sell the old one that keeps breaking down? There is nothing like walking everywhere in the rain and taking the bus to strengthen your desire, motivation, and resolve.

By now, you trust yourself, right? By now, you know that you are guided, right? You know that even after giving something all you've got, the universe can insist on pointing you in a different direction, so you know that you have what it takes to handle the temporary setback. And you know that when one door closes, a better one opens. This is so because you believe it to be so.

The only way to accomplish greatness in this life is to pursue your dreams and goals with undiluted fervor—the kind of determination that comes only from knowing there is "nothing to fall back on."

Most of us are raised to take the cautious route through life. Blah! Business leader and best-selling author, Bob Proctor, has a great saying: *I like living on the edge. If you don't, then you are probably taking up too much room!* I love it—I'm with him!

Be Bold. Be Courageous. Burn the bridges that provide you with an option to retreat.

You will astound yourself.

~*Tips for Plan A*~

- Have a single-minded focus. Once you make a decision to pursue your particular goal or dream, write it down and commit to it.

- To succeed at something phenomenal you must have a burning desire. Nothing says burning desire quite like having nothing to fall back on!

- Trust yourself. Shit happens in pursuit of all dreams. Know this: You have what it takes to deal with it.

- Dwell on the end result of your particular goal or dream. Imagine the finish line. How will it feel to get there? See it. Feel it. Savor it.

- If you want something bad enough, pursue it without options. Offering yourself options will dilute your desire, your determination, and your resolve.

- According to Anaïs Nin, *Life shrinks or expands according to one's courage.** Be courageous.

- Know that you are supported. Have faith. Stay connected to your Spirit. (See Rule 2, "There Is a Divine Intelligence").

You have what it takes to make your dreams your reality. Never ever dilute your dreams by planning escape routes. Trust yourself and make no Plan B. Burn your bridges. You will find a way when you have to.

What a thrill!

---

* *The Diary of Anaïs Nin*, volume 3, 1939–1944

Talk to Strangers

Do not neglect to show hospitality to strangers,
for by doing that some have entertained angels
without knowing it.

—HOLY BIBLE,
King James Version

My Story: Sex and Sugar Pie

F orgive me, the quintessential heathen, for using this quote from the Holy Bible, but it is so perfectly appropriate for the message at hand. Take heed of the words and give up being self-conscious, stuck-up, snooty, or shy. You are missing out on meeting people who have the ability to change your life. Tune in to your intuition, trust your instincts, listen carefully to your gut, and if the coast is clear, you *must* talk to strangers.

As a new immigrant painstakingly searching for my first "real" job in Canada, I paid a visit to a headhunter—a young woman also from my African motherland.

"I have nothing on my books to suit your background right now, but I'm attending a tradeshow this weekend and could use some help. I'll get you a ticket for the event in exchange for a few hours of your time at my booth. You can spend the rest of the time networking," she said.

Networking? I didn't know exactly what that meant. It sounded very North American to me and, frankly quite ominous.

"Uh, I'm not too sure what you mean by networking," I said.

"Just wander around and talk to people. Ask them about their line of work. Ask them for advice. Ask them if they're hiring. Talk to strangers."

I felt uncomfortable about this networking thing, but hey, I desperately needed to find a job. I walked up to a travel agent's booth; I loved to travel so maybe I could get a job selling or marketing travel. I started to chat to the girl manning the booth. She was about my age, tall and slim, with very short blonde hair and a big welcoming smile. The minute I started to talk, she cut me off, saying, "Hey! You're from South Africa! I grew up there too!"

After chatting for a while and offering advice on the jobs I should look for in travel, she asked for my phone number.

"Do you know anyone here?" she asked.

"I know one couple!" I said.

"OK, I'll call you—we can have dinner. I'll introduce you to some people."

I had no expectations. She was a busy woman, married, with plenty of friends and a full-time job. Two days after our first meeting, she called and invited me to a BBQ at her home. I was thrilled to get out of my sad little apartment and I jumped at the chance for company. The evening was fun, and within a few weeks Sonya and I were best of friends.

Her support and friendship through those early days of unemployment, have remained invaluable to me ever since. Now, twenty-two years have passed, and we have been through a few husbands and numerous lovers, jobs, careers, fortunes, and misfortunes together. We have stood by each other, laughed and cried, and together have come close to causing a worldwide shortage of wine.

In a single encounter with a stranger, I went from being a lonely, new immigrant who ate too much ice cream while alone on my couch every night, to having a group of friends who loved and supported me. It was their support that got me through my darkest times.

Ah, yes, how essential it is to life that we talk to strangers!

In February 1993, the month that my money would officially run out, I landed the job that saved my skin: district sales manager in cosmetics. Some of my training would take place in Montreal, and on one of my trips to that fabulous city, I decided to take full advantage of sightseeing opportunities. I extended the business trip and moved into a youth hostel for the weekend.

It was August and I took a break from walking the cobblestone streets and marveling in stifling heat and humidity at the old buildings. I went into an underground shopping mall for a blast of air-conditioning and a drink.

A hot Frenchman approached me. He was tall, dark, handsome, and dressed in black leather.

"Can I help you find your way?" he asked with a strong accent. He pulled up a chair and motioned to ask if it was OK to join me.

"Sure," I said. Actually, I kind of stammered; he really was bloody stunning. I sat at a little plastic table, drinking a soda, and poured over my maps and guidebooks.

"Perhaps I show you some good places?" he asked. He circled a few lesser-known spots on my map and lingered for a while. Before disappearing into the cool depths of the underground mall, he said, "Maybe you join me for some music in the park tomorrow—I will be at the angel statue at two o'clock. I wait for you. Maybe you will come."

That was it. I didn't even know his name, but I knew a good thing when I saw it, so I showed up at that stone angel at 2:05 p.m. the next day.

There he was, waiting for me. We sat on the grass and listened to music, not talking much. Monsieur Chaud was the kind of man who didn't feel the need to fill in long silences. Non-verbal communication and a sense of connection felt more comfortable to him than incessant chatter. Besides, he really did struggle with English, and my French extends to Bonjour, Merci, and in this case, "Oui." Very definitely "Oui."

"You are hungry?" he asked, after a while. "Come to my house—I cook for you." His voice was low and mellow, as though he occasionally had things to say, but didn't feel the need to force people to hear him.

His only mode of transportation was a motorcycle, and I smiled as I noticed a small helmet attached to the back seat brought in anticipation of my willing spirit. My father's angry voice lecturing about boys on death machines chipped into my brain, but only for a second. I climbed on and clung to the back of this stranger as he drove carefully through the streets of Montreal to his little apartment on Sainte-Catherine Street.

I sipped white wine and watched Monsieur Chaud cook for me in his tiny kitchen with its black and white checked floor. The aroma of garlic sautéed in butter and wine filled the French atmosphere, while scratchy recordings of Edith Piaf and Josephine Baker played on an old cassette recorder. The meal, like him, his clothes, and his apartment, was humble but stylish and seductive—so deliciously seductive.

After dinner, we played LPs on a turntable in the living room until 3:00 a.m. It went without saying that I wouldn't be going back to my hot, cramped bunk bed at the youth hostel. Forever the romantic gentleman, Chaud only touched me gently and held me close while I spent the rest of the early hours in his bed. He could feel my nerves; he was experienced, perceptive, and intuitive, and knew he had to take it slowly. We kissed. "You are so beautiful," he said.

He dropped me back at the youth hostel at 8:00 a.m. so that I could catch my early flight back to Vancouver. He held me and kissed me tenderly. This time we swopped numbers and addresses before saying goodbye. I was tripping on clouds; Chaud wrote me love letters. They came every few days and they were beautiful—flawed, genuine, vulnerable, *and* beautiful.

"You give me a demonstration of charm, intelligence, and sensitivity, and every second of time passed so quickly with you. I never expect to meet someone like you." He ended the first letter with: "If you want to see me again, just let me know and I will be your chevalier-servant." Holy shit.

During our initial meeting, I had mentioned to Monsieur Chaud that I would be in Montreal "once in a blue moon." He asked me what that meant and I explained. As it turned out, it wasn't long before I announced another visit, and in his letter dated August 24, he wrote:

Dear Jacquie,

I want to invite you to stay in my home for your blue moon trip . . . maybe you prefer a hotel but anyway my house is yours and if you stay, I am going to give you five-star service. It is just that I want to spend every second with you because the last time we saw each other was too short. The first time I saw you, I was thinking, 'do something – don't let her go – if you don't do something you're never going to see her again.' And now, I am really proud of me because it took all my courage to let you know that. I never expected that you'd be receptive to my advance. Of course the first time, I was stimulated by your beauty, but after that I was impressed by the beauty of your mind and your spirit. You meet great people once in a blue moon in your life so you have to say something. Don't waste time—say that you like them very much. I like you very much.

The most romantic weekend of my life occurred about seven weeks after I first met Chaud. He borrowed his father's truck to pick me up from the airport and we headed into the woods north of Montreal to the little rustic log cabin that he shared with his dad. On the way, we stopped at a grocery store to pick up basic essentials like coffee, champagne, and traditional Quebec sugar pie. It was late September, the fall colors were beautiful and the night air chilly and fresh. I think we drove for a couple of hours, and by the time darkness fell, we were making our way along a small overgrown dirt track. I was nervous with anticipation, and for the first time since I met Chaud, I felt a brief moment of extreme vulnerability. *What if he turns out to be a psycho?* I thought. *No one would ever find me.* Movie scenes flashed in my head.

Then the first bit of magic—we came around a blind corner in the road and almost ran into a large bull moose. He covered the entire track, so we had to encourage him to move before we could continue on. He was so close I could have reached out and touched him. This was heady stuff for a young South African immigrant fresh off the boat—in the dark North American woods with a hot Frenchman and a moose.

The cabin was in complete darkness and remained that way; there was no electricity or running water. I don't recall eating dinner that night. All I do remember is a beautiful man feeding me champagne-soaked grapes and, of course, making love on the floor all night long.

Monsieur Chaud was a sensual, generous, and gentle lover. He had to be—the man was hung like a horse. I mean, his dick was in a word, *humungous.* I remember the first time I saw it. Even in repose, I would swear that in my memory it hung to his kneecaps. *Fuck me!—I wonder where he's going to put that!* Looking back, what pisses me off is that I was relatively sexually inexperienced at the time, and plagued with all the insecurities that come with being a young woman (see Rules 1 and 4!), so I couldn't enjoy his spectacular piece to its full potential.

The next morning, by the time I awoke, Chaud had boiled kettles of water on the wood stove and filled a small, galvanized steel tub. Then he bathed me—he frigging bathed me! Afterward, he served me coffee and sugar pie. I have never tasted anything so perfect in all my life. God, I felt like a star in a French film.

That day, the air was chilly and filled with the smell of wood smoke. We strolled arm in arm around the nearby lake. The sun was filtered, and the leaves crunched under our feet. We passed quaint old cabins, and Chaud introduced me to some of his woodsman friends. I noticed how quick he was to tell them that I was from "Afrique du Sud" for fear that these Quebec Separatists would think that a good Separatist like him was dating an English Canadian. I was fascinated. Why do such ingrained beliefs still resonate with a younger generation? I am always fascinated by what makes people who and what they are. I try to understand why they believe what they do, no matter how unacceptable it may be to me. It's why I love to travel, another reason to say "Yes!" more often, another reason to get to know strangers. There will be no peace in the world until there is understanding.

The next time I saw Chaud, I began to pull away. His attitude and mindset were too poor for me, and the large chip on his shoulder ensured that he would stay that way. He had no ambition and scoffed at any suggestions I made to pursue opportunities. At my age at that time, I was uninterested in taking on a cause—it took enough for me to try and figure out my own purpose on Earth. I lost respect for him, and with that, I no longer desired him.

The circumstances under which our relationship ended were not good. He came to Vancouver and I refused to see him. I had met someone else at a bar in Whistler—a power-tool salesman from the 'burbs. Chaud was extremely hurt. When I look back at his letters now, I feel sorry that I hurt him so deeply; he was very sensitive. He viewed our connection as much more than just as lovers, and felt that even though I'd met another guy, we could still stay connected. I couldn't do that. One day, I received a photograph in the mail of him in the snow on Grouse Mountain. It had only the date on the back—no other words. I felt guilty and sad.

I often think about Monsieur Chaud, his kind soul, his extraordinary talent for romance, and his spectacular dick. I only wish that I had had the maturity back then to go along with his wish of remaining connected, despite the fact that I was hanging out with someone else. I feel blessed to have known him. I feel blessed to have experienced such beautiful romance and to have known his kind and gentle soul. I feel blessed to have experienced that magnificent dick.

And I am exceedingly grateful for the lessons he taught me. He inspired me to be courageous. As he said in one of his beautiful letters, *The first time I saw you, I was thinking 'do something—don't let her go—if you don't do something you're never going to see her again.' And now, I am really proud of me because it took all my courage to let you know that.*

And, *You meet great people once in a blue moon in your life so you have to say something.*

I try to remember his words of wisdom when I hesitate to talk to a stranger.

We pass by this way, in this form, but once.

Get up the courage to talk to strangers. They can open up your world.

~*The Lesson*~

The main reason that we don't talk to strangers, I think, is because we fear rejection. What if they ignore me? What if they yell at me to leave them alone? When you think deeply about this, why would it matter? And besides, the best way to approach this rule is with a smile. If someone smiles back and seems open and friendly, that's your cue to say "Hello" or perhaps ask a question.

Of course, most of us are taught from a young age to fear strangers and never to engage them in conversation. That's a fine sentiment to live by until you reach adulthood, at which time you should be tuned in to your own intuition and smart enough to follow common sense rules. Don't engage a stranger on a dark, empty street. Don't get into a car with a stranger. Steer clear of strangers who appear under the influence of drugs and alcohol. Never ever ignore your gut.

Here's the point: you'll never meet people if you stay home. Have your coffee in a coffee shop once a day, or a few times a week, rather than at home. Having lunch at home alone? Try a café instead. You never know when you will meet a life-changing character.

I engaged with a stranger at a trade show and she became my best friend. I engaged with a handsome young stranger in a grocery store and he became my husband. I've met lovers on airplanes, customers in the dog-park, and friends in coffee shops. I tune in and listen to my gut. When red flags wave, I know that I have to brush off a particular stranger, and I do it in a kind and respectful manner. Most strangers don't bite. Talk to them.

~Tips for Encounters with Strangers~

⊚ Get out of the house. Join clubs, gyms, and hang out at coffee shops .

⊚ Travel to safe places on your own. You will be amazed how many more people you meet compared to travel with a companion.

⊚ Smile a lot. You can tell a lot about someone by the way they respond to your smile.

⊚ Strangers will make contact with you if you give off a friendly approachable vibe. Look up from the newspaper or book now and then and smile at people.

- Compliment people. If you think someone is wearing a pretty dress, or has a great look, tell them. We all love compliments. Why not make someone's day? A compliment is so easy to give. If you're thinking something good, then say it out loud. (Well, not if it will get you arrested for sexual harassment, but you know that, right?)

- Be comfortable with receiving compliments. Smile, look confident, and say "Thank you!"

- When approached by a stranger, make it your first instinct to smile and to be nice. You'll need a moment to tune in to your gut. Red flags? Walk away politely into a crowd, or put your head down into your book. Use a kind excuse. "I must run—I have a meeting. (or my husband is waiting for me, etc.) Nice to meet you! Bye." There are numerous kind ways to bow out.

Talking to strangers is one of the most proactive, life-altering things we can all do on the road to a bigger and better life.

Have fun with it!

Rule

8

Heed the Signs!

*We often discover what will do,
by finding out what will not do, and probably he who
never made a mistake never made a discovery.*

—SAMUEL SMILES

The Lives of George and Robert Stephenson

My Story: A Gay Wedding

As I have already indicated, my first marriage was pretty darn bizarre, and you would be forgiven for wondering why the hell a straight woman would marry a gay man—and one with serious issues to boot.

But here's the thing. The year was 1994 and Mr. Merc swept me off my feet. He had a beautiful furniture store, rich clients, designer clothes, penthouse in the sky, convertibles, and cell phones. He took me to expensive restaurants that I'd never been to in cars that I couldn't afford. He was handsome, flattering, flamboyant, entertaining, and when he turned it on, he was the most charming human to have ever crossed my path. He referred to me as the "South African Princess," which, let's face it, was a huge step-up from the more accurate "poverty-stricken immigrant."

I had been in Canada for two years when we met, and I was still working my ass off in Vancouver as a district sales manager for the large direct-sales cosmetic company. It was high-pressure stuff: sign up five new reps a week, or get the warning letter. One of the company trainers flew in from

Calgary to work with me, and when I picked her up from the airport, she said, "I just sat next to a man that you have to meet. He is a successful businessman, handsome and charming, and when I asked him why he isn't married, he said that it's because he hasn't met the right woman. I told him that I knew the perfect woman for him! You! He gave me his card and said you should call!"

At that point I was dabbling with the geographically undesirable power-tool salesman. One day, he drove me past his future "dream house"—a little bungalow in the 'burbs. I recoiled. I was ambitious with big glamorous dreams, and I wanted a guy who at least aspired to live the same way. Where the hell was that contact card for the hot businessman with the penthouse? I drove home, sent a break-up fax to the power-tool salesman, and called the handsome businessman.

"What are you doing right now?" he asked. "Come over to my store, and we'll have coffee!"

I'll never forget the moment when he walked toward me for the first time and took my breath away. He was tanned, had dark racing eyes, dark hair, and long eyelashes, and his energy filled the enormous room. He wore a beautifully draped black Armani suit and flashed a thick wad of hundreds as he gave instructions to his staff.

"Let's go across the street," he said.

We talked in the little coffee shop for two hours. "My parking is about to expire," I announced. "I've got to go."

"No, don't go, let's talk more," he said. He ran out into the pouring rain to plug the meter. He was so interested in everything that I had to say, in my stories, my childhood, my country, and in me. He was impressively knowledgeable about South Africa and I was captivated right back. "Let's do this again soon," he said.

The next time meant a spontaneous dinner at one of those restaurants that had, until then, seemed untouchable to me. He had given me just a few hours' notice and showed up with great style and aplomb in a black convertible BMW at my ratty little apartment. Mr. Merc was always spontaneous and over-the-top, and very few people ever said no to him. We would all drop everything to go along for the extravagant ride. It occurred to me that our first two dates were the only times that we were ever alone; he liked to surround himself with throngs of people. He was a showman in the kitchen, and dinner parties at his penthouse were great spectacles of abundant food, alcohol, and laughter. Merc was treated like a rock star at the restaurants we frequented and, as his entourage, we felt pretty damn special by association.

We had dated only for about a month when he announced to me, in the kitchen of a friend's house during a dinner party, that he was in love with me and wanted to marry me. Really? Well, damn! What was not to love? Life with him was a blast—copious quantities of wine, vodka, laughter, lobster, notoriety, and luxury. I felt spoiled to a fault, doted on, and crowned a frigging princess. All the while, he seemed so kind, so generous, and so loving. Why the hell would I say no?

A few weeks after proposing, he went on a buying trip to Italy. He would call and tell me about the magnificent furniture that he had ordered "for us." He would tell me how much he loved me and how he couldn't wait to get home and spoil me. He arrived back with a big white box wrapped in red satin ribbon. The card on it read: "To the South African Princess, Can't wait to see you in this Ferré original! Love always, M." Inside the box lay the stunning off-white suit by Gianfranco Ferré—an ankle-length, fishtailed pencil skirt that fit like a second skin, and a gorgeous, short jacket, fitted at the waist, with loose bracelet-length sleeves adorned with large, round, embroidered buttons. Its design was extraordinary, and for a fashion-crazy immigrant who couldn't afford a new T-shirt, it was intoxicating.

Then there was the time that he bought me a horse—a beautiful, tall, bay thoroughbred. One morning during breakfast, he started to quiz me about horses. "I know nothing about them," he said, "but there is one that I'm interested in, and since you are an experienced horsewoman, I'd like your opinion. Let's go up to my friend's farm tomorrow and you can tell us what you think." I thought it was strange that a guy who didn't know how to ride wanted to check out a horse, but who was I to question what rich dudes did with their money?

When we arrived at the farm, the beautiful horse was already saddled up and being held by the supposed owner. "Jump on him," Merc said. "Ride around a bit." Never one to pass up the opportunity to get on a horse, I did as I was told. I walked, trotted, and cantered around the ring a few times then walked Star back to the gate where Merc stood with a few friends. Everyone was beaming.

"What do you think?" he asked.

"He's lovely." I replied, still sitting in the saddle.

"You look so beautiful on him. Do you love riding him?" he continued. I smiled and nodded and patted Star's neck.

"That's good," he said, and held a glass of champagne up to me. "Because he's yours!"

Dear God, I was blown away.

"Let's not go home tonight," he said. "Let's go and visit Mike in Whistler, and go out for a fabulous dinner and stay the night there. We have so much to celebrate!"

I was still in dirty riding gear and I didn't have any clothes to change into, so I protested. "Don't worry about that, Princess!" he said. "I have a plan."

When we arrived at his friend's house in Whistler, Merc handed me a robe and suggested I get cleaned up. "I just have to go somewhere quickly," he said. "I'll be back soon." He disappeared.

When I got out of the shower, he was standing in the living room with shopping bags full of sweaters, pants, and fur-lined boots—gifts, all for me.

I was beginning to *feel* like a princess. I felt that I was special, the chosen one put on a pedestal, and I could do no wrong. Ah, always beware of the pedestal—it's used to distract from hidden truths.

On the flight heading down to South Africa for the wedding, my pedestal started to wobble and sway. For the first time, I saw nastiness in Merc that I never had witnessed before. He snapped at me for no particular reason, and spent the majority of the exceptionally long flight talking to strangers. It became obvious that he wanted to avoid me. I sat by myself and felt a dark loneliness throb through my chest. I knew that there was more to this than met the eye. We were on our way to get married. The whole idea no longer could remain a fanciful fantasy for him. Reality had set in, and he snapped like a caged lion. I found out later that he had met the man of his dreams a few months before the wedding. Now he felt trapped by his own temerity.

Oh, there had been signs of trouble in the jovial principality—there are always signs. At one point a friend had called me to tell me that Merc was a serious cokehead, and what's more, everyone around town knew he was gay.

"WHAT? But he loves **me**, he wants **me**, he's marrying **me**," I said. "How could that be possible?"

I faced a major dilemma. Somehow, I had to confront him with this story; but what if it wasn't true? How do you "accuse" a straight man of being gay, and a clean man of being a drug user without him being furious? Besides, what if it *was* true? I was terrified of the answer. When I found the courage to confront him, I decided to replace the word "gay" with "bisexual" and to leave out the drug story completely for another day. We were going out for dinner one night and I asked for a few minutes to talk before joining our friends at the restaurant. We drove down to the beach and sat in his car staring out at the ocean. By now I was totally vested in being the princess and couldn't face the possibility of going back to poverty-stricken persona non grata. I shook like a leaf.

"What is it, Princess?" he asked. "You know you can talk to me about anything."

Oh, God. "People are saying that you are bisexual," I blurted out.

He turned his entire body to face me, took both of my hands in his, looked at me with tenderness that I can only describe as love and said, "Well, what they say is true. I am attracted to men and to women. When I am in love, the person's gender does not matter to me, and I am in love with you. I have never met anyone like you before, and I just know that we're meant to be together. I love you, and I want to marry you."

Well, that sorted that out. I *was* the chosen one—how frigging fantastic. I put my crown back on my head and heaved a sigh of relief. When it came to the drug rumors, I didn't care. He never did cocaine in front of me or even mentioned it to me. I was the chosen one, the protected one, the rescued one. I wanted to be the princess forever, and besides, I've always hated "normal." I had never wanted to be a wife, but a spoiled princess was just fine with me.

And now the wedding day had arrived, and the little ignored signs were about to be replaced with giant red flags waved in desperation by the Universal Spirit. The pseudo-celebration took place on December 17, 1994; it was a beautiful hot, sunny summer day in my African motherland.

I sat trussed up in my white taffeta meringue dress in the back seat of my dad's old cream Mercedes, and felt a tad queasy—motion sickness no doubt, from teetering on my swaying pedestal.

Shortly after joining the main highway that runs between Durban and Johannesburg that would take us to the town of Hilton and the old stone chapel of my high school, we came upon a wall of emergency vehicles. All of the traffic travelling between the country's largest port and its largest city was diverted off the double highway and onto an adjacent single-carriage farm road. We crawled behind large semis, farm tractors, vacationers, sales reps, oversized loads, and donkey carts. I felt beyond stressed. And yet, here it was: red flag numero uno being waved with a vengeance by the Mother Universe—a closed road! And what did I do? I put my blinders firmly in place and deliberately soldiered on. I was going to walk down that aisle, goddamn it.

By the time we arrived, storm clouds had gathered on the hot horizon and I was two hours late for my own wedding. The congregation had heard about the carnage and numerous fatalities on the highway and was happy to see that my dad and I were alive. The groom? Maybe not. He might have been praying that his ship had come in, that I was dead, and he would be free to go back to Canada and his new lover. I trembled as I held on to my dad's arm and floated toward the altar in a denial-induced trance.

Red flag number two was delivered with universal fury. The preacher was finishing her sermon and preparing to deliver the vows when the heavens opened. A mighty African hailstorm, accompanied by gale-force winds, pounded the tin roof of the old stone chapel with deafening conviction. I kid you not—no one could hear a word. Not a single word. The preacher continued. We leaned forward to read her lips and dutifully repeated the soon-to-be-annihilated promises.

I swear to God, the hailstorm began just before the vows. "Hello, Jacqueline. This is the Great Spirit, the Universal Force, The Creator, God, Whatever. Is there anyone there? Run, run for the hills, do not pass Go, do not collect $200, just run, run for the hills!" And this is what I did: I fortified my armored suit of denial and pressed on.

Now we were married. The hailstorm ended, the sun came back out, and we posed for photos. It was as though the Great Spirit, exhausted from strategizing and waving red flags, sighed and said, "What the hell—I tried. She's a stubborn one. I'll need to regroup and teach her a few lessons."

And so we made our way down to the Maritzburg Country Club for the reception. All that I really needed at that point was one glass of champagne before I succumbed to the immense weight and pressure of my suit of denial, and passed out cold in the back office of the club. I came to as my mother was stripping off my meringue, my hose, and my corsets. There I lay, buck-naked on the hardwood floor, while my wedding reception went on without me.

"Darling, some of the old folks need to go home, but they're all waiting for the first dance," Mum said. "Can you stand up?"

I was still shaky, and I put my hands on her shoulders to steady myself as she bent down and slipped the meringue over my feet and pulled. The corsets, panties, trusses, and hose lay in a pile on the floor. I slipped on my white wedding shoes and staggered out into the hall.

Once again, my guess is that the poor groom held out hope that I had miraculously disappeared for good. "Where have you been?" he asked.

Well, nice of him to notice. "Oh, just passed out in the back room," I said.

"Ah, well, hope you're OK. Let's get this dance over with."

"I'm totally naked under this meringue." I whispered, as we swayed to the music. No reaction. Let's face it—my anatomy did nothing for the guy. I can't even remember the song. Geez, what bride doesn't even remember *the song*?

After the honeymoon from Hell, we went back to Canada, and six stressful and devastating months later, it was all over.

~*The Lesson*~

Our Spirit Guide shows us signs. At first, we feel little flashes of intuition—gut feelings. When we continuously ignore them, trouble starts brewing. Slowly at first, but soon it amps up until we're pelted with more than we can possibly ignore. Continue to ignore the pelting shit and pretty soon your life can get quite screwed up. Yes, indeed—I learned my lesson. Heed the signs!

Of course, one has to be tuned in to the Divine Force (see Rule 2) to be aware of one's intuition, and at the time of this story, I was not. I was too busy running around as a shallow physical being with no connection to my soul and our collective spirit. The intuition part stayed totally lost to me. It wasn't until the actual physical signs, together with people stating the obvious, that I registered any awareness. And at that point, I took denial to a whole new level. My desire to check off the marriage box and to be a spoiled princess squashed any and all sense in my confused brain.

So I'll say it again—being tuned in and trusting of The Divine is crucial for happiness, joy, real love, and success. As is being your own soul mate! Do you think for a second that I would have been so gullible and downright idiotic if I had loved and trusted myself above all else?

One of my favorite quotes and lessons from Dr. Maya Angelou is this: *When someone shows you who they are, believe them.* So often we make excuses for people because we want to justify our own choices. We want so badly to believe the good in everyone, and we want so badly to be right. I would have avoided many hurtful or detrimental romantic relationships, friendships, and business associations had I applied this lesson throughout my life.

Now, here is something really important. Don't assume that every major challenge on your journey to a goal or a dream is a sign that you're on the wrong path. Shit happens and most of the time we have to plough through it. Nothing worthwhile comes easily, and you *will* encounter rough patches on your journey to greatness. **If you are perfectly honest with yourself and tuned in to your soul, you will know the difference.** If you remain in denial and run around fuelled by ego, you'll never get it.

On the flip side of this story are the positive signs that the Universe shows us—opportunities to pursue. My all-time favorite book about following the signs is *The Alchemist*, by Paulo Coelho. Many see its main message as one about finding your personal legend, but for me, the primary message is that once you start the ball rolling, the universe conspires with you, and shows you the signs to follow. Follow and do your part, and pretty soon, you *will* find your own personal legend.

~*Tips for Heeding the Signs*~

- Tune in to God , or The Creator. Be quiet, and listen to your soul. (See Rule 2.)

- *When someone shows you who they are, believe them.*—Dr. Maya Angelou. Don't make excuses for people.

- Be Your Own Soul Mate (see Rule 1). When you are you own soul mate, you will not hesitate to trust yourself. Your decisions will no longer be based on what others think or say.

- By all means, indulge in some crazy stuff but know when to stop. Going along for a wild ride can be a blast, but in my case, it would have made sense to stop before planning a wedding. Egos may have been bruised, but no one would have been so hurt.

⊙ Know how to diagnose denial. If you refuse to give any thought **at all** to negative consequences, you are in denial.

⊙ Sometimes rumors are simply rumors, but most of the time where there is smoke, there *is* fire. When your reputation, your heart, or your business is on the line, you would be wise to follow up on stories and rumors.

⊙ It's critical to know the difference between a rough patch, a lesson or a challenge, and a giant, waving Stop sign. When you are free from denial and dialed into your intuition, you *will* know the difference.

Once again, the message is *tune in and trust*. Don't wait for the pelting shit before you decide to heed the signs!

Be Frigging Fabulous

Style is more important than substance, initially.

—SEAN COYLE

The 25 Indisputable Laws of Style

My Story: Hindsight is 20/20

OK, so what do I mean by this rule? I mean you have got to be the best you that you can be. You have got to take charge of the things in your life that are within your control. Let's not kid ourselves; life rewards action, and society rewards fabulousness. When we think we look good, we feel good, and when we feel good, we go out into the world and naturally attract the people, circumstances, love, and opportunities that further our goals and dreams.

It is true that in Vancouver during August of 1999 I randomly met a man in a French Bistro who would change my life and my fortunes forever. I felt good that night, and I *looked* good. I had been reading self-development books, setting goals, was back to running on a regular basis. I had just started a new job that paid me a bunch more money than the previous one, and I felt phenomenal in my outfit. My nails and lips were red and I wore a black crepe, knee-length pencil skirt with a side slit, a thinly striped, shimmering black and white cropped top, and my favorite high, black strappy sandals.

I was with two gay men—one a best friend and the other an acquaintance. The maître d'–owner walked us to our round table by the fireplace at the end of the rectangular room, and I was aware of all the heads that turned as I strutted past. Don't you just love those occasions when all the stars seem to be aligned, the world is bright with possibility, and you instinctively know that something good is about to go down?

We were sipping our cocktails and pouring over the menu when the maître d' came back to our table. "Do you know Clara Marie?" he asked me.

"Yes," I said, "but what a strange question; she's a Zimbabwean girl who spent a year or two in Canada and is now living in South Africa. Who's asking?"

"Oh, just one of the patrons," he said mysteriously, and disappeared.

After ten minutes or so curiosity got the better of me and I took a walk toward the front of the restaurant to see if I recognized anyone. As I approached the door, a man sitting at the bar reached over and grabbed my arm. "Jacquie!" he said. "It's me, Ian Raynor."

"Oh, my God! Ian!" I said. Now it made sense—I had met him years before through Clara Marie.

"How are you, what are you up to these days? Meet my friend, Mr. Ferrari!" and he introduced me to the man sitting next to him.

Mr. Ferrari was expensively dressed, but stuck in an era gone by, with tassel loafers, a navy blazer complete with pocket 'kerchief, and grey flannels bedecked with about eighteen pleats running across the front. He didn't take his eyes off of me, even while Ian was talking. His stare was cocky and intense. He was intrigued by me and attracted to me and he wanted me to know it.

God, I thought, the guy's got balls. Does he even realize how *old* he is? I was thirty-three, and this dude was definitely in his fifties, so I brushed him off and went back to my table where my endive salad with blue cheese and candied walnuts waited.

I was sipping a glass of Pinot and tucking into my main course when Ian came over to our table. "Jacquie, we're leaving," he said. "Give me your contact details so we can meet for coffee and catch up one of these days." I handed him a card.

The very next day, Ian called me at work. "Actually, I'm calling you on behalf of my friend, the one you met at the Bistro—Mr. Ferrari," he confessed. "He wants to call you. He's a very successful businessman in the financial industry, rich, and you'd have a nice life with him."

Holy shit—if nothing else, I felt shocked and, frankly, a little insulted by his presumption. "Are you married at the moment? Single? Dating?"

"I'm in a relationship—have been for two years," I answered.

"Oh well, I had better tell him not to call then," he said.

"Yes, that would be best." I hung up feeling flattered but determined that rich, cocky, old Mr. Ferrari was not my type. Besides, even though my two-year relationship with an eccentric local plastic surgeon was hitting the skids, it was not officially over yet.

Presumptuous doesn't begin to describe these men, because even after telling Ian about my relationship, he gave Ferrari my number. And Ferrari, even after hearing that I was spoken for, devised a scheme and called anyway.

"I hear that you work for a Laser Refractive Surgery company," he said. "I had my eyes lasered by one of the docs at your clinic and I'm having vision problems. I need you to tell me what I should do about that." I informed him about company policy and told him how to go about getting a retreatment. We chatted for a while and then he said, "Look, I hear that you have a boyfriend, but I'd really like to take you out for a cocktail, so if and when you lower him over the side, you call me."

Turns out he had 20/20 vision.

Months went by. One night I was out to dinner with a large group for a friend's birthday, and I was seated next to the husband of one of my girlfriends. "Where's Dr. Porsche?" he asked.

"Oh, we broke up about a month ago," I said.

"Forgive me for saying this Jacquie, but I'm actually quite pleased to hear you say that. You see, none of us thought that you guys were really well suited and besides, I've been wanting to introduce you to a few of my friends in the financial biz for a while now. In fact, the guy that I played golf with today is someone that I think you should meet."

What the hell? I didn't know Rob that well, and I never imagined him as a matchmaker, especially not for me, but I felt touched by his interest in my dating wellbeing. He went on to describe Mr. Ferrari.

"Hold on just a second!" I yelled. "You're in on this too! This Ferrari dude won't take no for an answer and now he's even got *you* working on his behalf!"

"What the hell are you talking about?" Rob asked, with a genuine look of puzzlement.

"Well, this guy is determined to date me, so he gets friends to quiz me about my marital status, makes up stories about his vision so that I take his calls, and now he has you pretending to be some innocent matchmaker!" I said.

"Listen, Jacquie," Rob protested, "I swear on my life, I know nothing about this back story. I really, really am just an innocent matchmaker. I swear. It's the God's honest truth."

The "coincidence" could not be ignored and I decided that it was time for Ferrari's tenacity to pay off. I would, at the very least, go on one date with the guy. Rob suggested that they throw a Christmas party and invite both of us. It was kind of him, but after all that had gone down so far, I felt that the best approach was the direct approach. "I'll take it from here," I said.

I called Ian the next day and told him the latest restaurant story. Within hours, Mr. Ferrari called. "I know this is bold," he said, "but I'll be going to my home in Arizona for Thanksgiving and I'd like you to join me."

I should not have been surprised; naturally, this was par for the course for the man. I refused. "I have eight friends coming over to my place for turkey dinner."

"Cancel it," he announced.

"No," I said. "I will not." And so began a long and meaningful relationship between two pig-headed, strong-willed, attention-seeking, egoists that lasted for ten years and resulted in a complicated life of love, lessons, luxury, laughter, multiple homes, misunderstandings, and millions of dollars.

There are so many reasons why my relationship with Ferrari ended after a decade, and I've often thought about all the things that I could have done differently that may have changed the outcome. Life unfolded for both of us as it should have and I know this: nothing (including love) has to last forever to be perfect.

I am aware of the judgments and jealous opinions of many of those who knew us, and of the many who carry scathing criticisms of where my financial security comes from. I have worked hard to get to the point where I no longer care, but occasionally, I still become defensive. It was a great day for me when I realized, not with some scant belief, but with a deep knowing, that I am responsible for where I am at any given moment in my life, whether good or bad. And that doesn't take away from the deep gratitude I feel toward Ferrari, and others who have contributed to what I have, who I am, and the lessons that I've learned along the way.

My gratitude to Ferrari stretches way beyond my possessions, my bank account, and the invaluable relationship lessons learned from all the missteps we both took. You see, Ferrari believed in me like no one else ever has. He told me so many times over the years that I am intelligent, intuitive, smart, and capable. He told me so many times and with such conviction that I eventually started to believe him. After decades of self-doubt, and the subconscious belief that my success depended on being with a man, Ferrari convinced me to begin to believe in myself. He convinced me to believe in my own power and my own unique abilities.

My life had been in the doldrums a few months before I made the changes that led to my meeting Ferrari. I was in a dying relationship, living paycheck-to-paycheck in a small rental apartment, and working in a dead-end job. I began to study self-development and put into practice what I learned. I had a dream and a vision, and I started to set goals. And, most important, I never for a moment thought or wanted my salvation to come in the form of "rescue by man." I fully expected that it would come from a business opportunity, a new career, or a best-selling book, but the universe knew that I was not ready for those things and had other plans. I did my part and the universe decided to give me love, lessons, and wealth all rolled up into one.

I had started the ball rolling toward success by being clear about what I wanted in my life and by taking charge of the things that were within my control. I worked hard on becoming fabulous, and becoming fabulous worked for me. It will for you too.

~*The Lesson*~

This rule may seem shallow to you, but I think that people too often use excuses to avoid the work required to be fabulous. It takes time, effort, and commitment to look your best. As my grandmother, Gigi, used to say, "Anything that is worth doing is worth doing *properly*."

When you look good, you feel good. When you feel good, your attitude improves and you begin to attract what you need at each stage of your life. To change your attitude means changing your life. This is powerful stuff not to be dismissed. To become a magnet for opportunity, and to live an extraordinary life, you must do what you need to do to look good and therefore to *feel* good.

When you feel healthy, fit, and attractive, you will naturally come across as self-confident. Your self-confidence will attract people and circumstances that can catapult you toward your dream life. You will feel capable and radiant. You will begin to respect yourself, and as I mentioned already, self-respect is essential to self-love. And since our thoughts and beliefs create our destiny, your positive feelings about yourself will guide you down the path to greatness.

The universe responds when we begin to take charge of all the things in our lives within our control. It is up to us to start the ball rolling toward our dream life. Once we do that, the Force begins to guide that ball down the right path by presenting us with circumstances and opportunities. Nothing happens if we don't start the ball rolling, and keep the ball rolling, by taking constant action. Being as fit, healthy, and attractive as we can be is an essential place to start.

When you are your own soul mate (i.e., authentic and fulfilled) *and* you are fabulous? Wow! Look out, World!

~*Tips for Being Fabulous*~

⊚ Get fit and healthy. Exercise every day; don't kid yourself, it will change your life. Follow the 80/20 rule when it comes to food and drink. Eat healthily most of the time, but not all of the time. Be bad enough to be scintillating company and have some fun. Who wants a teetotalling, dogmatic, piqued, caffeine-free vegan as a dinner guest? Go to www. jacquiesomerville.com to get your copy of *My Fat Little Rule Book*—my irreverent look at food, fashion, and fat.

⊚ Develop a sense of style—enlist the help of those in the know.

⊚ If you're stuck in a style rut, educate yourself with magazines, and open your mind to what's current and fashionable. I'm all for individuality as long as it's creative rather than boring and *stuck*.

⊚ For those of you over forty, stay in touch with current events and popular culture. You will never be fabulous if you stay uninformed with a closed mind and stuck in another era.

- Take pride in your appearance and in your possessions. Keep your home and your car clean and neat.

- Don't mess with cheap expendables. You will feel cheap, portray cheap, and stay cheap. Always buy the best quality that you can afford. Less really *is* more.

- Be organized.

- De-clutter your home, your closets, and your desk. Throw away the crap and give away the decent stuff.

- Take action to change what needs to be changed. Hate your job? Do everything in your power to change it. In a detrimental or abusive relationship? End it.

- Be kind, have fun, and smile *a lot*.

Work on yourself! Be the best you that you can be. You will be doing your part and the universe will start to conspire with you. You will begin to get out of your rut and your life will begin to excite you! Do it. Be fabulous *now*.

Rule

10

Pursue Your Purpose

There is no greater gift you can give or receive than to honor your calling. It is why you were born. And how you become most truly alive.

—OPRAH WINFREY

"Honor Your Calling," *Oprah Magazine,* June 2011

My Story: Shine the Light

The loneliest I have ever felt in my life was on one day when Ferrari and I were together in our country home.

I felt depressed. But I had everything—a spouse, multiple beautiful homes, horses, and designer duds. We travelled in absolute luxury, ate at the world's finest restaurants, and drank rare wines. Ferrari spoiled me with bling from Cartier, bags from Chanel, and wheels from BMW. How the hell could I justify feeling so empty? So I beat myself up even more.

Man, I felt screwed up. I had all the big things, but I wanted the little things. I wanted Ferrari to walk past me and grab my ass from time to time. I wanted him to go kayaking spontaneously with me at sunset. I wanted him in the kitchen with me while I prepared dinner—perhaps to chop garlic beside me sometimes. I wanted him to ignore his phone and his email occasionally for a weekend and focus on me, on us, on our relationship. My wifely duties felt like a job and I hated that. I always had loved cooking and managing and organizing our homes. I did it for us, out of love, and for the love of our life together. Now, we no longer seemed connected, and I felt as though I performed mind-numbing duties in exchange for my extravagant life.

I had no identity. I felt as though Ferrari needed someone, anyone—not necessarily me—to handle the personal side of life while he got on with making pots of money and being fulfilled by massive business achievements. A career as a wife with love and connection is fine, but a career as a wife—no matter how well paid, in my personal opinion—without the love and connection, is a thankless, mindless, and unfulfilling life. Where had the love gone?

Once again, just as I did as a kid, I turned to solitude and my animals for sanity. I needed to be alone. When Ferrari was at one of our homes, I'd be at another. I developed a kind of rich person's paranoia—you have the perfect life but spend your days worrying about the things you have no control over. I fretted over global warming and pollution, and the ever-growing human population. I lay awake at night worrying about the extinction of wildlife and the ever-decreasing wilderness. These are all noble causes, and I was already doing my part as an individual. But lying awake at night worrying about what everyone else might be doing wasn't helping anything.

Ferrari was dumbfounded, and understandably so. He felt that he had given me everything I had ever wanted, so what the hell was wrong with me? I could never articulate well enough, without sounding ungrateful, my need for a loving connection as well as a career outside of the home. We went to counseling. It didn't work. Ferrari felt that he already had done everything right. He believed the least that I could do, for all that he had done for me, was to get on with my wifely duties and do them graciously. I was miserable.

Being at the mercy of a man for my complete lifestyle and livelihood was not what I was born to be. (See Rule 1.) Once again I had sold myself short and taken the easy route. I let old beliefs, self-doubt, and inadequacies dictate my life. I needed a purpose. I didn't know what to do about it, so I continued to sabotage my relationship in a subconscious desire to force change.

And force change I did. One day in 2009 Ferrari announced that he felt I no longer loved him. I started to backpedal. What had I done? Perhaps I *could* be happy being an invisible wife. Why couldn't I force myself to be happy playing second fiddle to an important man? But it was too late.

I had burned the bridge and now felt scared to my core. I had been unemployed for ten years. How was I going to make it on my own? All my old money tapes played in my head. "I'm useless with money. I'm not good at making it, only at spending it. I'm not an entrepreneur."

But I had forced my hand. Now I had to figure it out. I had run out of excuses and options and had to find my purpose. Now I truly felt destined to become the person I had believed I needed to marry in other words, a financially independent, strong, capable woman who was finally fulfilling her destiny.

I spent every waking moment trying to find "it"—that elusive thing called *purpose*. I plunged back into my self-development studies and devoured books looking for answers. I meditated, studied, and asked the Great Spirit for guidance.

I replaced some of the negative stuff with phrases like:

"What is needed is on its way."

"I expect miracles."

"Have absolute faith. It is impossible to fail."

These words filled me with strength and hope.

I also relied heavily on the wisdom of my life coach, Clarity. She followed up on one of our sessions and sent me a copy of the well-known excerpt from Marianne Williamson's best-selling book, *A Return to Love: Reflections on the Principles of 'A Course in Miracles'*

Our deepest fear is not that we are inadequate.

Our deepest fear is that we are powerful beyond measure.

It is our Light, not our Darkness that frightens us.

The author goes on to say "Your playing small does not serve the World."*

I sat at my desk reading these words over and over again with tears pouring down my face. It occurred to me that I had been "playing small" for years. I cried long and hard and I began to speak out loud to my Creator. I expressed gratitude for the difficult time I was going through—for the

---

* Marianne Williamson, *A Return to Love: Reflections on the Principles of 'A Course in Miracles'* (New York: Harper Collins, 1992).

fear and uncertainty. "I am fully aware that I have been liv-ing a half-baked life for many years." I said. "I needed this kick in the pants to force me to do what I was meant to do. Please give me peace of mind and please guide me."

I needed to quit being afraid of my own light. I needed to stand tall and proud and strong, and I needed to become *all* that I was put on this earth to be.

And step number one was to find out what that really means. At that moment, my purpose became finding my purpose. I felt fulfilled simply in the pursuit of the answer. I kept at it. I trusted that it would come to me one day. I asked for guidance and never stopped looking. I started a "Life-style" blog.

"But how are you going to make money from it?" peo-ple asked.

"I'm not sure yet," I said. "I'm putting things out there, and I believe that as long as I keep doing and trusting, the answers will come to me."

I took to heart the words of Dale Carnegie:

> Inaction breeds doubt and fear. Action breeds confi-dence and courage. If you want to conquer fear, do not sit home and think about it. Go out and get busy.
>
> *Dale Carnegie's Scrapbook:*
> *A Treasury of the Wisdom of the Ages*

Over time my blog began to reveal answers to me. The postings that resonated most with my readers touched on self-development—more so than my musings on fashion and my tips for a fabulous dinner party. They responded to postings that motivated them and to advice that empowered them.

"What am I good at"? I asked myself. "What do I love to do?" Eventually, I started to figure it out. I love to tell stories, true stories. I love to make people laugh. I love to perform and to inspire. I love to give advice when asked. I am driven to empower women. I love animals, chocolate, fashion, beautiful things. I thrive on uncertainty, and I am good at taking risks. I take plunges and burn bridges without needing to know the outcome. Except for the years of stability with Ferrari, my adult life has been defined by instability. While I could stand to learn how to embrace stability from others, I could certainly teach people to embrace more instability in their lives.

It came to me in small chunks over the course of two years. It came to me because I persisted. And here "it" is: My purpose is to tell my stories with humor and irreverence. It is to use my personal experiences to inspire women to take risks, to embrace change, to trust themselves, and to become all that they can be.

Now I had it, and I had to get on with it. Shine my Light, and in so doing give others permission to do the same.

Hallelujah.

~*The Lesson*~

Material possessions gained through any means other than pursuit of your purpose will never ever lead to long-term fulfillment. And I know that many people who are struggling financially don't care to hear that. They'd like to at least try it for themselves. I get that. They may well judge me harshly for my opinions on this subject and write me off as a rich whiner. I get that too. I'm merely sharing my own experiences with you—the truth as I see it.

Nothing will make up for ignoring your purpose, your reason for being. If you think you will be fulfilled only if you find a spouse, have a child, win the lottery, or get a new job, you're wrong. You will be fulfilled when doing what you're meant to do, becoming who you're meant to be, and making a difference in the lives of others. And making a difference doesn't necessarily mean being a philanthropist. A toy store operator fills a need and provides fun for kids. A convenience store operator fills a need and makes life more convenient for his customers. As long as you love what you to do, it's legal, and within your own moral boundaries, in all likelihood you're already making a difference in the lives of others, and you have undoubtedly found your purpose.

Perhaps being a wife and mother, or a husband and father, is your purpose. That's great, but once your kids grow up, you may well find yourself seeking again. And that's OK too, because the timing will be right for you. But the moment that you feel empty, or even slightly unfulfilled, make it your purpose to find your *other* purpose.

Finding your purpose means feeling whole. When you're whole, you attract healthy love and joy into your life. You will no longer meet people that you stick with for the wrong reasons.

Focus on your pursuit. Your thoughts will expand and develop into reality. You will start to find answers—some big, some tiny. Listen and act. Start the ball rolling and the Universal Spirit will help define the pathway. Circumstances will clarify your direction. You have to start somewhere. Take action.

Doing what fulfills you means waking up excited every day. It means peace but with a fire in your belly. And it means happiness.

Sounds fucking great.

Go for it.

~*Tips for Finding Your Purpose*~

- Begin by taking charge of the obvious things within your immediate control. Are you fit and healthy? Check out my book on the subject of diet and exercise—*My Fat Little Rule Book*. It's a great place to start.

- De-clutter your home, your closets, your car, your office, your desk and your life. You have to clear out old shit to make room for new shit and old ideas to make room for new ideas. See my blog posting on this subject, "Get Rid of Old Bag-Gage," by going to www.jacquiesomerville.com.

- Broaden your horizons by talking to strangers (see Rule 7), Opening your Mind (see Rule 12), and saying "Yes!" more often (see Rule 3).

- Read. Study. Ask questions. Seek answers from those who have figured it out.

- Ask your Creator for guidance every day. Express gratitude for all that you are and all that you have in this moment.

- Take up a new hobby, travel, take a seminar, or join a group. Open yourself up to answers and to opportunities.

- Ask yourself these questions: What do I love to do in my free time? What *things* do I love? What activities do I love? What am I good at?

- What causes are you passionate about? What do you want to change in the world?

- What did you dream about as a kid? What did you love to do that you no longer do because you are "grown-up"?

- What intrigues you even slightly? Research it further.

- What have you put off because you've been focused on "something to fall back on"? Change your focus, and dismiss the cursed "plan B."

- Ask your friends what they get out of your friendship. What do you offer others?

- Start before you are ready. Get on it. Live your life right now. Don't wait. Trust that you will be guided.

⊙ Never give up. You will find your purpose. You just have to keep looking, take action, and open your mind. Never give up.

As one of my mentors, Dr. Wayne Dyer likes to say, *"Don't die with your music still in you."*

Makes you think, doesn't it?

Rule
11

Take Responsibility

"By your own thoughts you make or mar your life, your world, your universe. As you build within by the power of thought, so will your outward life and circumstances shape themselves accordingly."

—JAMES ALLEN

From Poverty to Power

My Story: A Lemon or a Lesson?

Clarity is my life coach and my voice of reason. She guided me through the sad and scary time of my break-up with Ferrari and the subsequent complicated negotiations. I could have screwed up royally had I been left to my own devices and allowed anger and a bruised ego to dictate my handling of the situation. Instead, calmness and reason prevailed—for the most part. Ferrari and I were able to peacefully unravel what we had built up over a decade, without the intervention of the court, or even lawyers for that matter. I value Clarity and trust her advice implicitly.

As a part of my settlement, Ferrari bought me a brand new car. It seemed like the perfect choice for me—a luxury hybrid but with massive power. This meant cutting-edge technology, and Ferrari and I took the first two vehicles of its kind delivered to Vancouver.

The car looked beautiful—white with tan leather interior and a sexy shape. The engine roared with 480 horsepower when it needed to and switched to an eerie silence at very low speeds and traffic lights. Perfect for an environmentally conscious power merchant.

When MJC (Ms. Jacquie's Car) was a few weeks old, I was driving home from flight school (I'll explain later) when the engine light appeared and the onboard computer told me, with a sense of urgency, to go immediately to the nearest dealership and to drive there slowly. I did as I was told. The dealership said they would need to keep her for a day or two to diagnose the problem and arranged a loaner car for me.

Two days became three, then four, then five, and pretty soon two weeks went by. "What the hell is going on?" I yelled in frustration. "I mean this is a brand new super-expensive vehicle and it needs weeks and weeks of *fixing*? How can that be OK by *anyone's* standards?"

"This is a very complicated vehicle—we can't fix it so we have to fly a technician in from Germany to help us. We need another week," said the service manager. He spoke calmly, way *too* calmly for my liking. Didn't he see how incredulous this situation had become?

The technician from Germany came and went. Now we waited for a part. Every week, the guy in charge of the loaner cars called me to do a swap. They kept selling the loaners—it was inconvenient and I was mad.

After a month, my vehicle was returned to me and a week later wouldn't start. I was enraged. I waited in a smelly back alley for a tow truck and spewed vitriol over the phone to the dealership. After two more weeks of loaner cars, I demanded an alternative. I had a meeting with the general manager who informed me that my car was now fixed, but they would swap it for a new, fully gas-powered version if I refused to take it back.

He went into detail about the advanced technology of my active hybrid, and the fact that this amazing car actually cost the company double the sticker price to build. They were prepared to take the loss because the technology was so important for the future of automobiles. The gas model was cheap and ordinary by comparison, but the decision would be mine.

"What if I keep my car and it stops running again four months from now?"

"The offer will stand for a year," he said. "You can swap it for a new full-gas version anytime within the year." OK fine, so I decided to keep the car.

I drove as if on eggshells. Every time I turned on the ignition, I hoped that it would start and run properly. Whenever a light came on that I didn't recognize I held my breath. Maybe I should have swapped it. I needed to visit Clarity.

"Make peace with your car, Jacquie. You have to make peace with her, or she will continue to let you down." What? "She" was an inanimate object. What difference would it have made if I "made peace" with "her" or not? "It's *your* energy that is causing you grief. You need to make peace with her so that you shift the energy that you are putting out there to the universe. It's not the car, the company, or the dealership that's bringing you this stress and anxiety—it's you. Go and make peace with your car."

Yikes. I had learned this stuff from the spiritual gurus I study so diligently, but as we all know, it's so easy to nod in agreement when we hear words of wisdom and not as easy to actually put lessons into practice. I knew from what I had studied that everything is energy, and that if you look at an inanimate object under a super-powered microscope, you will see moving particles. Everything is energy—it just vibrates at different frequencies. I was vibrating at a pretty bad frequency and attracting bad experiences.

We've all had days where we get out of bed on the wrong side, and it never stops there—a series of calamities usually follow. I remember a classic day when I was in a big rush to get to an appointment. I felt flustered and aggressive from the moment I got into the elevator in my apartment building. I pulled out of the parking garage to find a dump truck blocking the exit. I ranted and waited. A few minutes later, I turned down my usual street to discover construction; the traffic had merged into a single lane from three, and I waited for two light changes to get through the intersection. All the while, I tapped my fingers and cursed. I pulled into the parking lot at the doggy daycare and ran inside to drop off my Jack Russell for some playtime. When I ran back to my car, I found the parking dude slipping a ticket under my windshield wiper.

I climbed into the car and started to laugh. Oh, my God, Jacqueline—you brought this on yourself! What a classic lesson, and you deserve it! From the moment I woke up, my bad energy had perpetuated a series of events. It was so obvious to me. I felt extraordinarily fortunate that my "lesson" would cost me only about $100 and not my life or someone else's. I try to remember that morning every time I leave the house in a rush or feel frustrated or angry. It's time to regroup, breathe, and vibrate at a level that attracts good shit, not bad.

The same day of my meeting with Clarity, I had a conversation with MJC. "I am really sorry for being such a dickhead, MJ," I said. "You see, I really do want you. I think you are fabulous and I am grateful for you. From now on I promise to only expect the best from you, and from now on, I know that you're going to serve me well."

MJC is now four years old and perfect. She has never had one other single issue. She gets routine services and oil changes, I keep her clean, and she looks just as she did when she rolled off the assembly line. I chat to her every day and tell her that I love and appreciate her. She is reliable, safe, powerful, and sexy.

Call me a kook—this stuff works.

~*The Lesson*~

One of the most freeing, life-changing realizations we can ever have is that we are responsible for our own lives and for the way they turn out. Conversely, there is nothing quite like blame to ensure a lifetime of ineffective misery.

I am the first to admit that some terrible things happen to people that are completely out of their control. I don't think that someone who lives a healthy life, but gets cancer because they were born with a certain gene, has brought that on themselves. The key lies in the famous *Serenity Prayer* that most of us know so well:

> *God, grant me the serenity to accept the things I cannot change, the courage to change the things I can, and the wisdom to know the difference.*

What we can do is take responsibility for how we *deal* with everything in our lives. We *choose* the level at which we vibrate. Send out positive energy and reap the rewards.

There are certain things that we have to accept, and accepting is very different from blaming. Blame is a horrible thing. There are two ways to rid your life of the poison called blame—one by taking responsibility and the other by forgiveness. If another person does something terrible to you, the only way to free yourself from a lifetime of stagnant torture is to forgive and take responsibility for your life going forward. Easier said than done for many people but utterly essential nonetheless. It's like swallowing a very bitter pill—difficult at first, but once it's done, the healing begins.

Forgiveness and taking responsibility are like so many other things discussed in this book: they are *decisions*. It's not complicated, and it's not rocket science. Make a decision from now on to take responsibility for how you operate, forgive those who have wronged you, and whatever you do, remove blame from your vocabulary **forever**.

Here's the reason why this rule is so cool. When you take responsibility for how your life has turned out so far, you realize that you are responsible for your future too. You are in control of your own destiny! When you know that you can be responsible for your *own* destiny, you will start to take action. You will no longer wait around for things to *happen* to you or for you. You will be more inclined to do what it takes to create a brilliant future, take a risk, rock the boat, and kick-start your life. You alone are responsible for it.

Accept, Forgive, Take Responsibility. Now you are on the path to greatness.

~Tips for Responsibility and Forgiveness~

- ⊙ Forgiveness is for you. It has nothing to do with the person who "wronged" you. They are responsible for their *own* lives. You are responsible for *yours*. Do it for you.

- ⊙ When you wake up in the morning, say this: "I am responsible for my own life. I will vibrate at a level today that attracts goodness." The level that you "vibrate" at essentially refers to the energy that you give off—your mood, your vibe. You are a like a magnet—you attract what you put out.

- ⊙ Create a daily routine that works for you so that you are not rushed. Create rituals that remind you to stay grounded—perhaps a nature walk, a prayer, or meditation.

- First thing when you wake up, stretch, drink a glass of water, and say, "Thank you for this day. Please guide me in everything that I do today."

- Make a decision to take responsibility for your past, your present, and your future.

- Catch yourself blaming and complaining. Replace those thoughts/words with: "I am responsible for my own life. I am in control of my own destiny!"

- From the moment that you wake up in the morning, be aware of your mood. If you feel rushed, frustrated or angry, stop yourself and breathe and regroup. Make a conscious decision to relax and to change your vibe.

- Meditate. Be still. When you feel connected to your soul, you will approach life calmly and be much more likely to forgive others and make peace with your challenges.

- Take action. Do what you need to do to be fabulous, to be productive, and get the ball rolling. Do your part, always be aware of what vibe you put out to the world. Make it positive. Don't ignore karma. It matters.

Make a decision to take responsibility for your life from this moment onward. Be grateful for all that has shaped you up to this moment. Know that you are loved, supported, and guided. You are in control of your destiny. It's so cool.

Open Your Mind Wide

Judging others makes us blind,
whereas love is illuminating. By judging others we
blind ourselves to our own evil and to the grace
which others are just as entitled to as we are.

—DIETRICH BONHOEFFER

The Cost of Discipleship

My Story: Robbing the Cradle

O n August 11, 2010, my Muslim boyfriend gave me up for Ramadan. I felt angry about his religion and especially about his decision to be celibate for thirty days. It would be one thing if he fasted and didn't drink alcohol for a month, but it was very difficult for me to not take the celibacy thing personally. "If you really love me and miss me as you say you do, then why would you "give me up" for so many weeks?" I asked.

Yeah, so, eventually I realized that it wasn't about me. And despite my contempt for organized religion, I conceded that The Holy Month was an important time for him to reconnect with his God, his family, and his culture. In actual fact, when I shoved my ego aside for a minute, I was in awe of his conviction and his deep confidence that I would still be around when the month was over.

I met Beamer in flight school. Yes, I did. When Ferrari and I split up, I knew that I wanted to do something significant with my life, but I still didn't know what that might be. As I mentioned in Rule 10, I was diligently seeking my purpose. I've always loved airplanes, and I wanted to know what it would be like to pilot a small plane. Satisfying my curiosity for flying seemed the perfect thing to do while I figured out my reason for being. I had the time, the money, and the interest, so I enrolled in flight school at the age of forty-four.

Our class was made up of a ragtag bunch of young men from all over the world, mostly from the Middle East. There was one Jewish dude from Israel, but the rest were Arabs from Egypt, Libya, Yemen, Qatar, and Saudi Arabia. Anyone who pretended not to notice this mostly Muslim group after 9/11 would be lying. I noticed but wasn't alarmed. I took them at face value, and they all seemed like decent young guys. Besides, it all made perfect sense. Many of their countries did not have good flight schools, if any, and English is the international language of aviation. A lot of students from around the world choose to study aviation in English-speaking countries so that they can become fluent by total immersion. There were two or three girls too, also foreigners, but not Arabs, as you can well imagine.

Beamer made a point of sitting next to me every day. If anyone else dared take his place, he would ask them to move. It became a running joke in the class, and the whole gang would warn any unsuspecting newbie to choose a different seat or face the wrath of Beamer when he walked in. I admired his impudence.

"We should go out sometime," he said, as I was about to pull out of the parking lot one day. "Give me your number."

We went out to dinner. After the meal Beamer asked, "What do you want to do now?"

Well, it was 10:00 p.m., and I was forty-four, so the answer appeared obvious to me. "Go home."

"You can't go home so early!" he said. "Come with me." He took my hand and led me down the street. We ended up outside a nightclub—one I used to frequent in my twenties. I hadn't been there in fifteen years. Beamer strolled to the front of the line and we were ushered in. We danced—he had rhythm and style. It was sexy.

And so began the very unusual relationship between a twenty-four-year-old Muslim man and a forty-four-year-old animal-loving, agnostic, ball-busting, financially independent woman whose best friends are mostly gay men.

I learned a lot from Beamer, not the least of which was to live in the moment. I wrote this after we had been together for a few months:

Sometimes.

Sometimes when my young lover lays his cute twenty-four-year-old head on my injured, worn, and frozen shoulder, I realize that it will be twenty years before his rotator cuff wears out.

Sometimes he reaches in for a tender kiss, and at about one foot from my face, I no longer recognize him through my blurred vision, and realize that it will be twenty years before he will need reading glasses.

Sometimes when my knee aches from too many years of jogging on pavement, I realize that it will be twenty years before he has covered as many miles.

> *And then sometimes, after we have passionately banged for the fourth time in a single day, I realize that it will be thirty years before he needs Viagra, and I tell my insecure, evil twin to shut the hell up and I go back to living in the glorious moment.*

Yes, I'd be lying if I said I didn't thoroughly enjoy being with a man twenty years younger than I am. Frigging awesome. And get this: I have no doubt that the universe already was opening my mind and preparing me for that twenty-nine-year-old that I would meet later in the grocery store—the one that I married.

Our relationship meant baptism by fire for Beamer. His beliefs and age-old paradigms were challenged on so many levels. Dogs are considered unclean in the Muslim culture, and my dog is my baby. He has free run of my home and the furniture, including the bed. It was a new and unusual experience for Beamer, but clearly being with me had become more important to him than worrying about canine cleanliness. I could tell that he was intrigued by Spencer's very obvious personality, and before long, they became friends.

Gay men dominated my dinner parties. Being gay is a "crime" punishable by death in many Muslim countries. "They are such nice guys," Beamer acknowledged. I knew that he was not about to change his deeply engrained beliefs overnight, if at all, but I could tell that my friends were making him *think* just by being themselves.

We argued fiercely about politics, religion, and social issues. I loved these battles. I could tell that Beamer never had been challenged this way before by someone that he liked and admired. I know that I had an impact on him even if only through exposure. At the same time, I learned so much. I was very interested in his country, his religion, his family, and his engrained beliefs. I came to understand much more about his culture, and I came to realize that we all come by our issues honestly. Understanding is critical to eventual peace in this world.

In June 2010 I went to Vegas for a weekend with my girl-friend. I went directly to the airport from flight school on a Thursday afternoon. I wanted to take my flight-training manual with me so that I could study on the plane and by the pool, but I had forgotten it at home.

"Don't waste money buying a new one," said Beamer. "Borrow mine for the weekend."

I settled in by the pool at the Four Seasons in Vegas, ordered a margarita, and opened the textbook. Beamer's notes were all over the pages and they were all in Arabic. There were names and phone numbers scrawled on the title page: Ahmed, Muhammad, Abdulla. "Holy crap!" I said to my girlfriend, Sonya. "Look at this! Thank God we weren't searched at the airport!"

Imagine being caught crossing into the USA with a flight-training manual annotated in Arabic. Holy crap! I'd probably still be sitting in a US jail trying to explain that one away. Beamer hadn't even given it a second thought.

He attended flight school because he loved airplanes and wanted to be a commercial pilot. He was Muslim and his language was Arabic. So what? "Yeah, well, after the horror of 9/11, you can understand their concerns, right?" I said. Another debate ensued, this time about conspiracy theories and hypotheses that made me mad.

Beamer and I ended our relationship after ten months. I needed to be free and unattached. He wanted more, and I couldn't give it to him. I needed to pursue my career goals without having to put the time and effort into a relationship. Quite simply, this where I was at that moment in my life, and it made us both sad.

Here's the thing: Despite our vast differences, I really, really like the guy. He has a good heart, is loyal to a fault, stylish and cheeky, and fun. He takes risks and pushes the envelope and I like that (no shit, Sherlock). He opened my mind. I realized that I *could* love and respect someone whose views made me crazy. I want to know if his views change as he ages. I want to know him ten years from now—and twenty. What would our discussions be like then? What will he have done with his life?

I quit flight school before getting my license. I had done enough to satisfy my curiosity. I knew what it took to fly a small plane and I could take off, fly around, and land (although, according to my brave instructor, I still landed like a "drunken sailor"). I also knew that flying was not my passion. I had challenged myself to learn something new and had scared myself in the process. It was a phenomenal experience.

By now I had figured out that my career lay in the business of personal development. I wanted to write books, tell stories, and to inspire.

I had to get on with it.

~*The Lesson*~

Here's what I've learned over the course of my life so far: Our lives are enriched by variety. Surrounding ourselves with homogenous people who think and act as we do is not only boring but incredibly stifling to our growth. Debate, dialogue, arguments, and discussions make us more thoughtful and intelligent.

Also, bigotry and hatred come from ignorance. We should not turn our backs on an opportunity to change people's lives through education, exposure, and by giving them the time of day.

I have also learned that judging others is a terrible thing, and yet we all seem to do it on one level or another.

I remember once flying from Johannesburg to Cape Town to visit my sister. She met me at the airport and we chatted excitedly while waiting at the luggage carousel. "Oh, my god, Caro," I said, "you have got to see this man who was on the plane with me. He is the fattest person I have ever seen in my life. He's so huge that he took up two seats. The flight attendants had to rig up a special seat belt for him. There! There he is!"

A man standing behind me tapped my shoulder. "You are talking about my best friend," he said. "And he is probably the nicest human being to have ever been born. He is a stellar man. And not only that, but he is also a massively successful businessman. You should think twice about your judgments of him, young lady."

Yikes. I felt as small as a mouse. My comments honestly had not been used for any derogatory explanations of the big man but more out of fascination and curiosity. I simply had been genuinely taken aback by his size and had wanted my sister to see him. South Africa back then was very different from America. Enormously fat people were rare. I still learned a valuable lesson that day, and one that I will never, ever forget.

We miss out on untold riches when our judgments prevent us from getting to know others.

Always watch what you say. You could be standing beside someone's mother, or a very loyal, best friend.

The world would be a bland place if we all looked the same, yet our judgments are often out of control when it comes to appearances. There is a transvestite who likes to roller skate around the west end of Vancouver. She's over six feet tall, with long, scraggly blonde hair, and she usually wears a pink tutu. She often sings as she skates and seems so happy. She warms my heart and makes me smile. I marvel at her courage to fly in the face of convention, and every time I see her, she reminds me to be myself no matter what.

The Skater reminds me to be grateful for all the unique and charming people who make up our beautiful world.

I love people who wear outlandish clothes and who challenge the stuffy status quo. Let's embrace the oddballs. They're the ones who have the guts to inspire change. They bring color and joy to the community.

The world has so much more to offer us than we are prepared or willing to acknowledge. Open up to it and judge not.

I wrote a blog posting entitled "Bad Judgment" that resonated strongly with my readers. Go to www.jacquiesomerville.com to read it.

Vive la différence!

~*Tips to Open Your Mind*~

- Catch yourself judging. Replace the negative by saying something like, "I am so grateful for variety, and the fact that we are all different."

- Tune in to your Divine Spirit and radiate love. You will feel less inclined to judge.

- Leave judging to the law courts. You will be much freer and happier if you do.

- Open your mind by reading books or articles that challenge your way of thinking.

- Talk to strangers! See Rule 7.

- Travel. See the world. Go to places that may make you a little uncomfortable. Meet the people that you ordinarily would not meet. You will begin to realize, for all our differences, that we all have the same basic needs. We all want to be heard, to matter, and to be loved.

- Visit the ethnic neighborhoods in your own town or city. Try different restaurants, different cuisines. Experiment!

- Give new things a good chance before you write them off. I hate opera, but I sat through a few tragic Russians slowly dying on stage before coming to that definitive conclusion. I am also rather a heathen when it comes to classical music, but I have attended enough symphonies to make an informed decision. I still won't turn down a free ticket, though; you never know when something fabulous will surprise you and change your mind.

- If you are over forty and stuck in a time warp, open your mind to the music, fashion, and culture of the younger generation. I'm not saying that you should dive right in and try too hard to be hip, but at least don't be critical. It makes me crazy when I hear people complaining about "the youth of today." Those who do are closed-minded old farts not only stuck in a rut but also in a cycle of complaining.

- Spend time with people from different generations. You will learn something and may just be very inspired by those much older or much younger than you.

- Be your own soul mate! See Rule 1. When we love ourselves, we are secure with ourselves. When we are secure with ourselves, we no longer require validation by having to be right all the time.

- Acknowledge that you are unique and special and a child of the universe. You deserve to be here and so does everyone else.

- Give people the time of day before you decide to write them off based on preconceived notions about appearance, politics, religion, race, or sexual orientation. You will discover so much more than meets the eye. You will be amazed at the joy that variety will bring to your life.

I do know that some people, while born innocent, become evil over time, and we shouldn't mess with them. Trust yourself. If you tune in to your instincts, you will know whether or not someone is evil. I don't for a second suggest that we embrace people who are violent or cruel.

The key is that through acceptance, we will hopefully catch some people before they get to that point.

Variety is the spice of life—embrace it!

Rule

13

Know This: Shit Runs Deep

I see too plainly custom forms us all;
Our thoughts, our morals, our most fixed belief
Are Consequences of our birth.

—AARON HILL

from *Zara*, a British tragedy performed in 1735

My Story: The Vegetable Thief

One night a year or two ago, I was tossing, turning, sweating, and fretting for hour upon restless hour—about money. I had some, quite a bit actually, but what would happen later if I had spent it all? What was I going to do if I never found clients to support my business, if my books didn't sell, if my dreams of a speaking career never materialized? After all, who was I to think that I could be a successful entrepreneur? I was useless with money and probably always would be. Well, useless at making it but bloody good at spending it. And hadn't I always been told that people were either born entrepreneurs or not, and that I was one of the nots?

And so I beat myself up with negative shit all night long, until a lightbulb sent from the Great Spirit exploded in my head. Oh, my God, Jacqueline, remember the lettuce story? You *are* a frigging entrepreneur—you really, really are! In that moment, I changed my long-held, ingrained, and stifling belief about money and me, and in so doing in that moment, I began to change the course of my life.

When I was a little kid, before we moved to the farm, my siblings and I would be given a nickel a week for pocket money. We went to the store after church on a Sunday and were allowed to buy frozen apple juice, a sort of pseudo icecream thing, and that was it—the end of our money and the end of our treats until the following Sunday. Crap, I thought. I want more. And so, at the age of six, I devised a plan to get more.

My mother had a spectacular vegetable garden. One day when no one was looking I selected six perfect lettuces, chopped them off at the base, and arranged them in an attractive basket. I set off down the street in search of neighbors in need of greens. I sold every lettuce for twenty-five cents each. Get this: I was now in possession of *thirty* times my weekly allowance! I hid the money in a little beaded purse at the top and very back of my closet. I spent it in tiny increments over the following months so that no one would notice.

Where did my idea come from? We had no TV in South Africa back then, and I had I ever been to the movies. My mother was a housewife, and my father was a salaried man. Can you say "entrepreneur"? (I realize that some may say "thief," but I would argue that at six years old, taking advantage of one's family's shared resources showed creative innovation and not criminal deviance!) I also have no doubt that my parents instilled the admirable concepts of innovation and initiative into us kids from day one.

And yet, all my life I'd been told by well-meaning people that I would be a good secretary. All my life I was told by people with good intentions that if I wanted my big dreams of owning a beautiful thoroughbred-horse farm, of being rich and free to choose to come true, that I would have to fall in love with a rich man. I was told that life is difficult, that money doesn't grow on trees, that you have to work like a dog and hang on to your money (or marry a rich man). Over the years, the little lettuce entrepreneur started to take this view of life as the gospel truth. The same person who had multiplied her income by thirty times in a single hour, began to believe that making money was extremely difficult, that she didn't have what it takes to create the life of her dreams, that her dreams and her happiness would depend upon her falling in love with a rich man.

And so it was that I spent the next thirty-five years of my life trying to find that little lettuce entrepreneur. It is no surprise that those years contained marriages and relationships with wealthy men. It's no surprise that I subconsciously chose crazy ones that couldn't last, or sabotaged the good ones. I didn't like myself much, and I was not doing what I was born to do. Who *was* this person and what had she done with the one who dreamed of being independent, rich and free, of making it on her own, of flying in the face of convention?

But here's the really important thing to understand: Those thirty-five years were not "lost" years at all. The beliefs that my parents held about money were *their* beliefs, born honestly from *their* upbringing and experiences, and it is my view that those beliefs were essential for me at the time. They were a vital part of my journey. This particular lesson about money and my purpose was *my* lesson to learn—a necessary piece of the puzzle that forms who I am and what I am supposed to become, and for that I am very grateful. You see, this rule has nothing to do with blame. This rule is about awareness, acknowledgment, and moving forward to your own version of greatness.

~*The Lesson*~

Ah, yes. The stuff drummed into us from a young age runs deep; pretty soon, the beliefs of others become our beliefs and determine the course of our lives. This may be all fine and good and meant to be, but it becomes our responsibility as we journey through adulthood to determine which of those ingrained beliefs hold us back and which support us moving forward into a purposeful, fulfilled, and happy life of our own. We achieve this by dreaming big dreams, by studying the beliefs of successful, happy people, and by reading and questioning. Eventually, we figure out which beliefs work for us, which beliefs to dump, and what we need to replace them with.

We cannot change what we don't acknowledge. We must delve into the past, because we have to know what our beliefs *are* in order to change them. We also have to know where they came from. Why? Because when you realize that your age-old beliefs are not carved in stone, but that you're merely parrot-phrasing theories passed down to you from other fallible human beings, albeit well-meaning ones, you're able to kiss the old beliefs goodbye. Now, you'll give credence to some fabulous new ones that can boost your life into the stratosphere!

If you're one of those people who feel stuck believing only a select few are born for greatness, and that you're not one of them, understand this: Recent studies on the old nature-versus-nurture debate have shed some mind-blowing light on the old belief that our genes and our environment work independently of each other, and that both have separate input into the shaping of our destiny. In fact, our genes interact *with* our environment and they work together to create who we are at any given moment in our lives. I find it exhilarating and enlightening to learn that our intellect and talent are not predetermined at birth, but rather are *processes* taking place over time as our genes and environment interact with each other. Of course, our genes play a role; however, given the right environment, we can *all* be great.

The consensus now is that most of us don't have any idea what our true limits are—we haven't yet come close to tapping into our full potential. In his book, *The Genius in All of Us*, David Shenk writes: "Most underachievers are very likely not prisoners of their own DNA, but rather have so far been unable to tap into their true potential. He also writes, No one is genetically doomed to mediocrity."

How cool! We actually can influence our genes! Let's make the necessary changes to our environment, our beliefs, and our old paradigms, so that we begin to positively influence our genes, "tap into *our* true potential," and move toward greatness.

Regardless of who gave birth to us or where or when we were born, we can all become great. We can even influence our *genes* by changing our environment, and we can change our environment by changing our thoughts and our beliefs. We all have the power to do so, and that blows my mind!

~*Tips for Change*~

- Embrace dissatisfaction! Without it, we would all bumble on in a state of mediocrity. Dissatisfaction promotes learning and growth.

- Be dissatisfied, but be happy! There is a big difference. If you are struggling to be happy in the face of dissatisfaction, start by counting your current blessings and smile a lot. Happiness is a decision—a state of mind. Like all decisions, you make it, and then you work at it.

- Question yourself. Why are you dissatisfied? What would change that? What does fulfillment look like to you?

- Dream BIG dreams. Let it rip. Don't hold back. Forget about what's practical and what you think you are capable of. Forget about reality, and make this a beautiful, magical, impractical, glorious fantasy—pure fantasy! What does it look like? Write it down. If this exercise makes you feel even more dissatisfied with your life, that's a very good thing! You will make changes when dissatisfied enough.

◉ Question why some people, but not you, seem to be living their dreams. After all, our gifts and talents are unique and different, but we were all born for greatness. What's holding you back? Could it be your age-old beliefs about how life works?

◉ Question what your beliefs are about money, work, deservingness, blame, your support system, love, friendship, luck, your value and talent. Which beliefs are negative and preventing you from greatness?

◉ Which beliefs make you feel as though good things happen to others and not necessarily to you?

◉ Where did you learn these beliefs? Could it be that they were passed down to you from fallible human beings, whether individually or collectively? Could it be that they held these beliefs based on their own unique set of experiences? Why would that apply to you? Who made up these rules anyway, and why do you accept them as the gospel truth?

◉ Read. Study. Question. Interview. Learn from people who live a life that you admire. What beliefs do they have that have enabled them to believe in themselves and to achieve greatness?

⊚ Adopt the beliefs of these people—the beliefs that make sense. Can you see how they differ from your own, and can you see what a difference these beliefs make? Create mantras and affirmations based on these beliefs, and start chanting. Yeah, I said chanting! Well, OK, call it "repeating," but say it out loud. I promise you, this shit works. It may seem kooky and out there, but if you don't do it, your old beliefs will keep you strapped to the treadmill of mediocrity.

⊚ An old long-held notion suggested that it takes twenty-one days to create a habit. Nowadays, the thinking is more like sixty-six days. Whichever is closer to the truth, you have to be consistent, disciplined, and repeat your mantras multiple times a day until the words become a belief, and the belief becomes a knowing.

⊚ Here are some examples of mantras for you to write three times a day: Repeat out loud three times in the morning, three times at night, and multiple times when alone in your car!

> Yes, I Can
>
> I deserve success
>
> I AM a successful entrepreneur
>
> I am talented and valuable
>
> I AM creative

I am good with money

I am loved and supported by the source of all life

I was born for greatness

I am smart and I am capable

I am kind and loving

I trust my intuition

Yes, I can—Yes, I can—Yes, I can.

⊙ Be grateful. Be grateful for your life, for love and support, for what you have, and for the awesomeness that is coming your way!

Repetition works. After all, you believed all the stuff that was repeated to you over and over again as a child, didn't you? Now it's your turn and your responsibility. Change your thoughts and your beliefs, and change your life.

Draw Your Lines in the Sand

We must develop and maintain the capacity to forgive.
He who is devoid of the power to forgive is devoid
of the power to love. There is some good in
the worst of us and some evil in the best of us.

—MARTIN LUTHER KING, JR.

From the speech "Loving Your Enemies," at the Dexter Avenue
Baptist Church, Montgomery, Alabama, Christmas, 1957

My Story: Despicable Me

I remember a conversation from 1989 in Johannesburg with my friend, Marley, about infidelity "I will never, ever sleep with a married man," I declared.

"Oh, don't be so sure," she said. "You should never say never."

Really? That's not how I was raised. I was raised with a strict moral code, but one that I've brutally challenged in my adulthood. And I'm not proud to say that in 2009 I began an affair with a married man. It continued on and off over the course of two years.

I met Bentley in the bar of a downtown Vancouver steakhouse on a passion-filled night fueled by lust and stress. It had been four months since Ferrari's announcement that I no longer loved him, and I had been banished to our ranch. I was no longer welcome in our Vancouver home, and I was spending a few days in a hotel with my friend and neighbor.

It had been four very stressful months mired in sadness, anger, and uncertainty while I hung in limbo waiting for Ferrari to make a decision.

I had told Ferrari that I would be prepared to change, to seek counsel, to do whatever it took to put our relationship back together, and to make it good.

"I don't know if I want to try to make our relationship work. I may not. I haven't decided yet. I need more time," Ferrari kept saying.

"OK, let's just end the damn thing—I want out," I eventually yelled uncontrollably. I wanted desperately to stop the pain and hasten the negotiations so that I could move on with my life.

"There you go again, trying to control everything. I'm not ready. You have to wait for my decision," he yelled back at me.

Well, what the hell difference would it make if he decided to work at it or not? By then, I really wanted out. I was sick of being strung along and putting my life on hold while he used time to punish me for whatever it was he blamed me for.

Our relationship was clearly over, but I think that it was the reality of negotiating a financial settlement that Ferrari was putting off. After ten years, with many millions of dollars, multiple homes, animals, and an expectation that we would be together forever, it was now very complicated.

That night in the steakhouse I was out with three girlfriends, drinking champagne, flirting, and letting off steam. Running had been my savior throughout months of desperate tension. Despite my internal turmoil, on the outside I looked pretty good in my skintight, charcoal, leopard-print dress and four-inch stilettos. Four men took up the barstools alongside us. Bentley was one of them and he was into me; he made no bones about it. It felt good to be desired after so much stressful anxiety. I felt reawakened. Bentley did not wear a wedding ring.

After a while at the bar, we were all shown to our respective tables for dinner. I went downstairs to the washroom, and when I came out, I found Bentley standing in the stairwell pretending to check his blackberry.

"You're very subtle," I said sarcastically.

"And you are absolutely stunning, just stunning, and I don't want to leave tonight without connecting with you," he replied.

"That's entirely up to you," I said. "Thanks very much, I'm flattered."

He sent champagne to my table. After dinner, we all hooked up again at the bar. Our flirting became so intense that I felt I was one suggestive comment away from a full-blown orgasm. I wanted him. I couldn't wait.

Bentley walked my girlfriend and me back to our hotel room. She wisely disappeared into the bathroom; he threw me up against the wall, kissing me passionately. There was a wet spot on my dress and it wasn't from him. I felt like I was going to explode. My friend drew out her brushing and flossing for as long as humanly possible. The reality was that I had a roommate. Bentley would have to go.

I didn't sleep at all, tossing and turning all night long. I might as well have been strung out on cocaine. Eventually, I got out of bed around 4:30 a.m. and went for a run.

Bentley and I met for lunch, and it was then that I found out he was married. I just came right out and asked him.

"Yes," he said. "But it's not good and I don't want to be." Isn't that what they all say? I didn't care. I felt like a runaway train.

It took another day for us to find the moment. My girl-friend kindly, and amidst hysterical laughter, agreed to stay in the hotel across the street. She had borne witness to all that I had been through in the preceding months and stayed non-judgmental in her support of my impending relief. Bentley showed up before work—at 6:00 a.m. I was ready for him: clean and fresh with a black La Perla bra and thong under my white hotel robe. Who was this woman, and what the hell had she done with me?

He rocked my world. I was ravenous. We fucked for an hour. He showered and went to work. I drove back to the ranch.

And so it was that an addiction was born. Bentley became a drug to me. I'd renege every time I decided that I shouldn't continue to see him. It was all about sex and being desired. I told him that if he ever left his wife for me, he'd be making a grave mistake. I needed to live alone. I loved living alone. I told him that even if the ghost of JFK Jr. arrived on my doorstep with a suitcase, I'd let him stay one night before asking him to find a hotel.

I didn't see Bentley during my ten-month relationship with Beamer, but the minute that it was over, I was back in his perfectly noncommittal arms.

And then I did something despicable.

I stooped to a new low. I slept with Bentley in his home, in his bed—the bed he shared with his wife. Her bed.

The next day I couldn't look at myself in the mirror. For days afterward I couldn't think about what I had done without feeling overwhelmed by self-loathing, manifested physically in debilitating waves of nausea. OK, Jacqueline. Face this. It happened, so you have to find out why. Where is the lesson? Find it. Acknowledge it and deal with it, I told myself. I had to find a way to forgive myself. And the way to do that would be to find the lesson in what I had done. I had to pick myself up out of the gutter, learn from it, and move on.

The truth is that for the first time in my life I really enjoyed being a bit of a floozy. I was forty-five, single, fit, adventurous, wealthy, and I felt sexy and free. Ah, but chronic narcissism comes with such things. The combination felt fabulous, but it was undoubtedly dangerous. It gave me the illusion of being invincible and able to do whatever I wanted.

Mother Universe stopped me in my tracks with a lesson that I couldn't ignore. Have fun, but don't lose yourself completely. Have fun, but have some moral boundaries. You will be brought down by your careless approach to your own standards. Set boundaries and stick to them.

You have *got* to draw your own moral lines in the sand, and for the sake of your soul, you have to stick to them.

I have no regrets about having the affair. Bentley and I were meant to meet. After a sexless and stressful few years, uncommitted sex was perfect for me. I finally felt strong and in control. I felt sexy and powerful. I felt like I was *finally* ready to become that person that I had been sidetracked into thinking I needed to marry. I have no doubt it worked for Bentley too on whatever level he needed it to. But will I ever do it again? Never. Marley was wrong. We *must* say never.

Now I know that I need to be crystal clear about my own boundaries. I need to set them and I need to stick to them.

I am grateful for the lesson.

~*The Lesson*~

If you feel tempted to judge me right now, I would ask you to consider these words from Paulo Coelho:

> We can never judge the lives of others, because each person knows only their own pain and renunciation. It is one thing to feel that you are on the right path, but it's another to think that yours is the only path.[*]

Figuring out your own lines in the sand is an intensely *personal* thing. You must define your own set of standards and your own moral code. What's right for one is not necessarily right for another. Be honest with yourself. Staying within the boundaries of the law is a no-brainer, but beyond that, what should you say "**Never!**" to?

Are you indulging in behavior right now that makes you feel unsettled? Can you look at yourself in the mirror and say that you're living an impeccable life based on your own

---

[*] Paulo Coelho, *By the River Peidra I Sat Down and Wept* (Harper Perennial, 1994).

standards? If not, I ask you to take the time to more carefully define what those standards are, write them down, and vow to start living by them.

So why do I have a rule about setting boundaries when the entire purpose of my book is to entertain you and to inspire you to be a little nuts? Let's go back to my favorite subject, "Be your own Soul Mate." You will never be able to love yourself fully, and therefore achieve greatness by *believing* in yourself, if you continue to disappoint yourself.

I'll say it again: Self-love requires self-respect. When you respect yourself, you will like yourself. When you like yourself, you're on the path to self-love. When you love yourself, you will trust yourself. When you trust yourself, you'll be able to take the risks necessary to live an extraordinary life. So yes, the irony is that we *do* need boundaries to be free to take risks— our *own* boundaries, the personal ones that work for us. We need to respect ourselves before we can love ourselves. When we love ourselves, fear and doubt no longer hold us back.

I also want to emphasize Rule 13 here: "Shit Runs Deep." Remember to distinguish between what has been ingrained in you by others and what's really, really right for you. Perhaps you feel uneasy about going against the grain rather than going against what's right for you personally. I ask you to reread Rule 13, and think long and hard about this.

It's OK to question society's standards. It's OK to question society's righteousness. Figure out what your own lines in the sand are and live by them. You get to define your own life and create your own destiny.

How are you doing when you look at yourself long and hard in the mirror? Look behind the eyes. Do you like what you see?

Yes? Now you are on the path to greatness!

~*Tips for Setting Your Personal Boundaries*~

- Analyze where you are in your life. What are you getting up to that is making you uneasy?

- Do you *believe* in yourself? Do you really believe that you can achieve your goals and dreams? If not, take a good look at how you currently live. Are you living up to your own standards on every level, including your own moral standards?

- Are there things about your life that you avoid? Do you bury your head in the sand about certain activities? Force yourself to face the truth. It *will* be hard at first, but tremendously freeing once you rid yourself of denial.

- What do you need to change in order to gain your *own* respect?

- Your lines in the sand don't have to be the same as anyone else's. Have the courage to define what's right for you personally. It really doesn't matter what anyone else thinks. Remember, those that judge do so because of their own shit, not yours.

- Need inspiration? Read *The Four Agreements* by Don Miguel Ruiz.

- Being crystal clear is a wonderful thing. Don't be ambiguous about your standards. Don't be afraid to carve them in stone. It really is good to say "**Never!**" when it comes to your own code of ethics. You'll like yourself so much more when you do.

- Don't judge others! This is a great place to start when drawing up your own code of ethics. They are responsible for their lives—you are responsible for yours and yours alone .

Set your own standards and stick to them unwaveringly. You will set yourself free. You will like who you are. You'll begin to love yourself, trust yourself, and you'll be able to move forward and take risks on your path to greatness!

Live Large and Dream Big!

Imagination is more important than knowledge.
Knowledge is limited.
Imagination encircles the world.

—ALBERT EINSTEIN

From an interview with G.S. Viereck,
"What life means to Einstein," *Saturday Evening Post*, Oct 26, 1929

My Story: Be Careful
What You Wish For

W hen I was a little girl riding my horse in those sugar-cane fields so far away, I dreamed of a big life. In my mind's eye, my big life was always overseas even though I could never face the thought of leaving my motherland. But that's OK because dreams should never deal with the "how." Dreams deal with the end result. Besides, I didn't have to face the reality of leaving because my dream was a wonderful fantasy—a thought that played like a movie in my head. I couldn't wait to go riding so that I could be drawn up again into my imaginings.

My dad went on a business trip to America in 1971. He had been to the Kennedy Space Center, to Hawaii, and to Disneyland. He told stories of the people he had met and the ice cream he had tasted. He loved the place and I was enthralled. I wanted to go to America. And from that moment on, while others dreamed of skiing in the Alps, being serenaded by a gondolier in Venice, or being awed by the Mona Lisa, I wanted to ride the rides and taste the ice cream. Those Americans sounded like a fascinating bunch and their country seemed like my kind of place.

And so I dreamed of visiting America. TV eventually came to South Africa in 1975, and I fell in love with Little Joe on *Bonanza* and, later, with *Magnum, P.I.* I visualized riding the range at top speed across the grasslands of the Ponderosa with Little Joe and helping Magnum catch the bad guys in Hawaii. Turns out my ideal men were handsome Americans with horses and ranches and fast cars.

By the time I turned twenty-one, I still had not been overseas. My wealthy friends regaled me with lavish stories of Europe—the old buildings, the culture, art, and history. I wasn't impressed. I wanted to take in jazz in New Orleans and soak up the atmosphere in Times Square.

Turning twenty-one is a huge deal in South Africa. Those of us who were fortunate had extravagant parties resembling weddings, complete with marquee, sit-down dinners for a hundred or more people, a DJ, and an elaborate cake. My pink-and-cream-striped marquee had been set up in the garden of my parents' home. My mother had decorated the interior with magnificent flower arrangements, and had made my cake complete with horse adornments. My party was held just after final university exams were written, and my close friends from school and the university were there. I enjoyed an awesome and memorable night.

We could drink, vote, and drive at eighteen, but twenty-one was considered "coming of age," and parents usually gave their kids a symbolic key to the door of life. My folks gave us three lucky kids cash to mark the occasion. We could choose how to allocate the money. I decided to have my party with some of my money, and the balance I would use to go overseas. America was out of the question. It was too far away and I couldn't afford the flights and hotels. I decided on a nine-countries-in-twenty-one-days tour of Western Europe.

Ah, but I hadn't visualized Europe for fifteen years; I had visualized America.

Your thoughts become your reality.

One day before booking my Europe trip, and quite by divine design, I met an American family from Massachusetts who offered me the opportunity of a lifetime: an air ticket to Boston and to live rent-free with them for six months, all in exchange for helping out with the kids and household chores. What? I could go to America? I could live there with a family and immerse myself in American culture? I could take some time to travel around? I gladly dropped my plans for the been-there-done-that tour of Europe. I was excited beyond measure. Now I dreamed about life in Boston. I was wild with excitement.

Jumping at this opportunity—despite being useless at ironing, vacuuming, and cooking—enabled me to live my dream. I made contacts, met travel companions, and explored America on a shoestring. I skied in Vermont, watched Baryshnikov dance *Giselle* in San Francisco, rafted the rapids of the Colorado river, ate rattlesnake in Missouri, climbed into the crown of Lady Liberty, threw a few coins into the slots in Vegas, drove on Route 66, rode the rides at Disneyworld, cried at Pearl Harbor and the Vietnam War Memorial, window shopped on Rodeo Drive and Madison Avenue, marveled at the Kennedy Space Center's rockets that had taken men to the moon, rode the range on horseback in Montana, took in the architecture of Chicago, the street performers in New Orleans, and attended concerts by the icons of the time, Tina Turner, Bruce Springsteen, U2, Madonna, David Bowie. I was in love with America and I didn't want to leave.

But, as you already know, I went back to South Africa in 1988 and moved to Johannesburg. Jo'burg was a wild and crazy place—a city that straddled the razor-sharp line between First and Third Worlds. It was a dangerous mix of speed and money and poverty and crime. I never settled. I was in my early twenties, and I would lie in bed at night worrying about my future. Would there be peaceful change to bring about the end of apartheid, or would there be a bloody civil war? The value of the currency had fallen rapidly as sanctions and intense labor unrest began to strangle the economy. What if my company decided to pull out and I lost my job? And then there was the crime rate—it was through the roof.

There was no end to the horror stories, and sometimes they happened just around the corner. A family who lived two streets over from me in the northern suburbs of Jo'burg had been tied up, the mother and daughter raped, and the house ransacked. The criminals, evil people who then slaughtered them all, were strangers to the family.

I too became the victim of a home invasion at two 'o clock one morning, and I will forever feel grateful that the man who entered my bedroom that night was only looking to steal. I was untouched, but completely terrified.

Our homes began to look like fortresses surrounded by electric fences that could blow someone to the moon. Carjacking became a national sport and almost always ended in tragedy. And we didn't see even the half of it. The government continued trying to perpetuate the myth of Nirvana. So many South Africans remained in a deep state of denial. "But there's crime in every country!" they would say. But not like that; there wasn't crime like this everywhere.

Denial was born of self-preservation. So many of us, myself included, were citizens of the Republic of South Africa with no access to a passport from any other country. My mind raced. I wanted so badly to go back to America, but America was full. They accepted only asylum seekers, refugees, family members, and some very special people in categories where they needed them. There was no immigration category for someone like me. I had to figure something out—I didn't know what, but as usual, I babbled on about it to anyone who would listen.

My dad, that resourceful and well-connected man, approached me with an idea. He had heard of a Canadian lawyer who recruited potential immigrants from places where people were desperately looking to leave. These included Hong Kong at the time and, of course, Johannesburg.

"Do you still want to leave this country so badly?" he asked.

"Yes," I said.

"Go and see this Greenfield chap. If he takes your case and you get into Canada, your mother and I will help you pay for the lawyer and your move, because one day, the whole family may need to benefit from your big step. You can pay half of the costs back to us once you are established."

It sounded like a deal to me. I felt sure that Canada would be very similar to the United States, which is where I knew I wanted to be. I also felt certain that I would use it as a stepping-stone to one day get back to America.

Thus, my association with Greenfield began, and on May 2, 1992, I became a very proud resident of the True North Strong and Free. Over the years I became one of the most patriotic Canadians. I fell deeply in love with my adopted homeland. I had found my place in the world. But it is a cold and wet place (on the West Coast, that is) so when Ferrari and I split up, I bought myself a vacation home in the California desert. I had the perfect life.

Ah, but be careful what you wished for long ago . . .

Remember the story about the young ex-con in the grocery store—the American man that I married? Under the circumstances, it would have made sense to date or live together until the relationship ran its course. It would have made sense to see what life was like with a thirty-year-old ex-con with a son and an array of "bros" either in prison, just out of prison, or having been in prison at some point in their lives. Yes, it would have made perfect sense, but par for the course of my life, I had to jump in boots and all, fly in where angels fear to tread, and throw all caution to the wind. You see, Bad Americans With Criminal Records are not allowed into Canada, and Good Canadians are not allowed to spend more than six months a year in the United States. It all makes perfect sense, but it really screws things up if you're a Good Canadian who falls in love with a Bad American.

Our options were few and far between: Break-up or get married, so that we could at least live in the same country. And since he's not allowed into mine, I would have to move to his.

Being apart for six months every year was not an option for us, and neither was breaking up. We love each other, and with my dog and his kid, we are a family.

And now I live in the land of the free. The True North still calls my name, and I miss my country and my friends more that they will ever know. I am, however, excited about my new adventure.

I feel like I've unwittingly come full circle. The universe has given me what I focused on and what I asked for over and over again, but has done so in its own time and with its own agenda. My job is to say "Yes!" to all the opportunities and go along for the ride. My job is to be bold, courageous, and fully alive. I wouldn't have it any other way.

So far my life has been one massive adventure. I could never have planned it like this, but I take responsibility for it all. Whenever it's too stable, I rock the boat. When the

Great Spirit sends me opportunities, I say "Yes!" When I want something bad enough, I burn my bridges. I talk to strangers with an open mind. I pursue my purpose with renewed vision, and as I do so, I know that I am supported and guided.

Oh, and now that I know how this whole thing works, I'm focusing on a Gulfstream VI. (And world peace.) Why wouldn't I?

~*The Lesson*~

Be careful what you wish for!

Dreams do come true even if you've forgotten about them for a while.

~*Tips for Manifesting Your Dreams*~

Here's how it works:

- Let your imagination flow. Create fantasies and visions. Play movies in your head.

- What did you dream about when you were a kid before society started to fill your head with limitations?

- Your movies should be fun and exciting, and they should not fall into the category of "realistic." Remember: What seems unrealistic to you at any given moment in your life can become a very definite reality down the road, so why limit yourself?

◉ Your Spirit Guide gets what you want and works with you to make it happen in the best possible and sometimes thrillingly convoluted way!

◉ You put it out there and then you say "Yes!" to the opportunities that come your way (after sensible consultation with your intuition, of course).

◉ Most of the opportunities will not seem like they relate to your ultimate dream. Say "Yes!" anyway. Remember: There are **no** coincidences.

◉ Set goals along the way. Goals are the achievements that take us in the direction of our dreams.

◉ In my case, I had the opportunity to meet with Greenfield. Setting goals and having deadlines for my residency application ensured that I got the application done well and on time.

◉ You must have goals because they perpetuate action. Sitting on your ass on the couch with a dream is useless. How will you meet with the opportunities if you wait on the couch? Go out and live your life to the fullest.

◉ Your goals don't need to be related to your dream, because you don't need to know *how* to make your dreams come true. Needing to know the "how" will make your dreams smaller than they ought to be. Make your ultimate dream pure fantasy!

- Your goals can be about becoming the best you can be. They can be about fitness, health, education, sales calls, job applications, and networking—the small things you need to do so that you're ready to run with the opportunities when they show up. You *have* to do your part.

- Share your goals and dreams. There are many "gurus" who warn against this, but in my experience, talking about my hopes and plans has been instrumental in making them come true. Someone may hold the key to an opportunity that will further your dream. Talk to people. And when it comes to goals, sharing them brings accountability into the equation.

- Sometimes the universe will take its sweet time, but it knows best. You are meant to experience all the peaks and valleys along your journey. Trust this.

- As long as you're doing your part, i.e., dreaming, setting goals, taking action, and trusting, things will unfold as they should.

- When the shit hits the fan, remember: There is a lesson in the challenge, no matter how brutal it may seem.

⊙ My main mantra in times of struggle is: "This too shall pass." Letting go and trusting that difficult emotions will run their course is very comforting.

⊙ Prepare to be amazed!

Dreams don't have to be material. In my case, I dreamed of a new country. I dreamed about being an animal philanthropist. I dreamed of being able to help family members in need. And I would be lying if I said I didn't dream about wealth and multiple homes and horses and a dog and a sexy man and a designer wardrobe. And I've been blessed with all of them. What are *you* dreaming about?

Start Dreaming. Start doing. Bust out of your rut. Be your own soul mate! You have everything that you need right within your own soul to become all that you were born to be. Trust your spirit.

I wish you love and good fortune on your journey. You deserve a fabulous life. Go out and get it.

I know this about you: You were born for greatness.

Believe it.

A Last Word

There is only one way to live an exhilarating life, and that is to do the work and take the risks necessary to live up to *your* full potential.

An alarming number of women over the age of 59 become alcoholics. In many cases, their husbands have either died or left them, and the kids have flown the coop. Their identity, life, and purpose were wrapped up in those who have left, so they find themselves broke, alone, and filled with regret.

In a 2011 *Guardian* newspaper article I read about an Australian nurse who worked in palliative care and had recorded the topmost regrets of the dying. Here is regret number one:

"I wish I'd had the courage to live a life true to myself, not the life others expected of me."

Most people hadn't even realized half of their dreams.

We can change these sad realities by realizing our own extraordinary power. We can change them by loving ourselves, believing in ourselves, and realizing that the most important thing we have to do on this earth is to find our purpose and live up to our full potential.

Don't hang your hopes and dreams on other human beings.

You are an individual with tremendous strength and power. You already have been given ALL that you need to become fully you. So use what you've been given to become all that you can be. Utilize your talents and realize your full potential, and one day when you die, it will be without regret.

I'll say it again. You are an individual with tremendous strength and power. Life is meant to be exhilarating, it's meant to be exciting, and it's meant to be a great adventure! *You* have the power to make it so.

Love others fully and with an open heart. Remember that nothing must last forever to be perfect. You are strong and powerful, so you are able to withstand failure and rejection. What matters is that you go for it—live and love all out. It's the only way to get to the end of your days without regret.

Here's my final message to you: Take risks, trust your intuition, work tirelessly on yourself, open your heart to uncalculated love, and then have some major faith. You are guided and supported by something greater than yourself. When you live this way, you will be challenged beyond measure, but great success comes from great challenges. Nothing great was ever achieved without adversity. Approach adversity with the knowledge that "this too shall pass" and with the belief that there are no coincidences in this world. Look for the lessons in your challenges—that's when you'll grow. It's often in times of hardship that we reveal the best of ourselves. Those who avoid failure and adversity avoid life.

You truly were born to excel. You were born for greatness. You have to push the envelope to get where you want to go. Challenge the status quo, and fly in the face of convention.

I wish you an exhilarating ride filled with love, wealth, adventure, and freedom.

Go out now, my peeps, and grab life by the balls!

Yes you can.

About the Author

Photo by Starla Fortunato

Jacquie Somerville isn't your typical motivator, author, or speaker. A born storyteller and a self-titled "normal-phobe," she probably will shock you and make you laugh.

Jacquie impacts her audiences by drawing on a lifetime of challenging and rewarding experiences—a lifetime of pushing the envelope, taking big risks and challenging the status quo. She's been married a few times, immigrated twice, been fat, slim, broke, rich, and followed her gut to a life of excitement, adventure, passion and purpose.

Jacquie's fearless approach to life and zeal for inspiring others to take action is grounded in a wonderfully diverse background, ranging from a successful career in corporate marketing and sales, to a degree in agriculture, to time in front of the camera as a main character on a reality TV show. An in-demand motivational guru, Jacquie has studied self-development in earnest for the past fifteen years, and has had the privilege of being mentored by some of the biggest names in the self-development world, including Brendon Burchard, Bob Proctor through his Matrixx program and Tony Robbins via Mastery University. Jacquie is also the CEO, personality, and creative force behind Jacquie Somerville Enterprises, LLC, a boutique self-development umbrella company for her keynote speech engagements, her banner "Be Your Own Soul Mate" online video program, her weekly "Jacquie Straight Up" inspirational video broadcast, as well as her books.

Jacquie's first published book, *My Fat Little Rule Book* is a fun take on diet and exercise, while *My Scandalous Little Rule Book* is a definitive guide to risk-taking and embracing uncertainty. Jacquie is currently writing *My Rich Little Rule Book*.

Jacquie was born in South Africa, immigrated to Canada alone in 1992, and now resides in Rancho Mirage, California.

To find out more about Jacquie and her life-changing products, to book her on your stage, or to sign up for "Jacquie Straight Up," please visit www.jacquiesomerville.com.